Connecting Through Circles:

Using Circles to Support Inclusion, Establish Belonging, and Build Trust

Cecilia B. Loving
and Gina Leow

Myrtle Tree Press

ALEXANDRIA, VIRGINIA

Myrtle Tree Press LLC, Alexandria, Virginia
Amazon.com – Authors' Pages:
Cecilia B. Loving and Gina Leow

Connecting Through Circles: Using Circles to Support Inclusion,
Establish Belonging, and Build Trust /
Cecilia B. Loving and Gina Leow — First Edition
Cover Design by Leo Estevez

ISBN 978-1-7364224-4-1 (hardback) |
ISBN 978-1-7364224-2-7 (paperback) |
ISBN 978-1-7364224-3-4 (ebook) |
Library of Congress Control Number: 2023923305

Praise for CONNECTING THROUGH CIRCLES

"*Connecting Through Circles* is about a method, a tool, and a process.
But it's more than that. It's about creating a human experience
that removes rank, station, and hierarchy.
It creates what I call cultural flatness.
In this container, people can model and reward vulnerability,
and in that process, share, listen, connect, discover,
celebrate, forgive, and change.
You're not the same person on the other side.
That's the whole point.
What a beautiful resource, Cecilia and Gina
have given us to bridge and heal!"

Timothy R. Clark, Founder/CEO of LeaderFactor;
Author, *The 4 Stages of Psychological Safety:*
Defining the Path to Inclusion and Innovation

"The medicine for shame is radical compassion, the loving presence
that helps us trust our belonging and essential goodness.
Cecilia and Gina's guide for circles calls forth this compassion and
helps us repair what's broken, listen for what's missing, and connect
with the common ground of our shared human experience."

Tara Brach, Mindfulness Leader
and International Best-Selling Author

"What our world needs urgently is people sitting in circles, sharing
their experiences with one another, with respect and trust.
This book is a wonderful resource towards making that happen.
I have had the privilege of sitting in circles with both Loving and
Leow. How fortunate for us all that they have come together to share
their wisdom, knowledge, and experience."

Paul Browde, M.D.
Narrative Psychiatrist and Couples' Guide
Co-Founder, Narativ, Inc.

"In a circle, there are no corners or edges. In much the same way,
Connecting Through Circles lends itself to an intimate and transparent
experience where everyone is moved to participate. Our firm was
fortunate to work with Cecilia Loving in 2020 during a particularly
sensitive time of racial and social tension across the country. Her use
of circle discussions created a safe space for our attorneys and staff to
connect on a personal level, which demonstrated her proficiency in
humanizing conversation to allow authentic exchange.
The impact of that work continues to yield benefits years later."

D.L. Morriss, Partner, Hinshaw & Culbertson LLP

Praise for CONNECTING THROUGH CIRCLES

"Having worked with both Cecilia and Gina forming and facilitating circles, I am excited for and proud of these strong women for expanding on the techniques that lead to foundational change through circle keeping. Restorative circles have been healing places that have allowed me as a trans person, oftentimes feeling pushed to the outside, to experience visibility, strength, and empowerment."

Brooke Guinan, FDNY Firefighter and Trans Advocate

"As a conflict resolution and restorative justice practitioner and trainer for over 25 years, I am grateful for the gift of *Connecting Through Circles*. Cecilia and Gina's story of how they integrate the use of circles to support engagement, inclusion, and belonging is essential—not only for leaders but for everyone who wants to make a difference in the world."

Elizabeth Clemants, Founder and Executive Director, Hidden Water

Praise for CONNECTING THROUGH CIRCLES

"This book is a fantastic resource for anyone looking to get started with implementing restorative justice circles. Specifically for inclusion and belonging or employment professionals, this book explains the importance of implementing restorative justice circles as a conflict resolution tool to ensure that staff feel valued and supported in their working environment. If you want to develop efficient teams that work together with trust, this book is for you."

Bayliss Fiddiman, Esq. – Civil Rights Attorney

"Cecilia Loving and Gina Leow have expertly captured in *Connecting Through Circles* what has sorely been missing from most DEIB corporate discussions and programs: intentional listening to one another as described in their book. I highly recommend *Connecting Through Circles* for all DEIB corporate executives and practitioners at every level of the organization who are working towards meaningful and sustainable positive changes within their organization."

Sabrina A. Griffin, DEIB Consultant and former Diversity Manager, Chubb Group of Insurance Companies

Praise for CONNECTING THROUGH CIRCLES

"A timely and illuminating resource
that feels like both a toolkit
and a love letter."

Veronica Agard, Practitioner and Curator, Ancestors in Training™

"Having read *The Power of Inclusion*,
where Cecilia introduces the concept
of using indigenous circles for difficult conversations,
I was delighted to find that *Connecting Through Circles*
provides a deeper dive into the importance of storytelling
and the history of how circles
have been facilitating connection and mutual support
through the ages.
I especially appreciated the book's discussion
about psychological safety
and how we can approach DEI work
with consistency, commitment, and courage.
Kudos to Cecilia and Gina for putting together
this piece that will no doubt
produce far-reaching benefits."

Jordana Confino, Founder & CEO, JC Coaching & Consulting

Praise for CONNECTING THROUGH CIRCLES

"Connecting Through Circles is a vital tool for your toolkit. This timely book provides Cecilia and Gina's unique view of how we can benefit from restorative circles for courageous conversations, emotional intelligence, healing harm, and resolving conflict. Whether you're in government, a corporation, a school, or any space where we have to bond with others, circles help bridge the gaps that need closing by requiring us to slow down, listen, engage, support, and sometimes even transform through our shared stories."

Ray Kramer, Adjunct Professor of Law, NYU School of Law, Mediation Clinic and the Advanced Mediation: Dispute Systems Design Clinic, and NYU School of Professional Studies, Conflict Management & Dispute Resolution

"Cecilia B. Loving and Gina Leow bring a wealth of experience and expertise from the DEI field to guide the reader in how to use the power of circles to bring people together with a simple, compelling, and proven methodology. This book is an empathy generator. By the time you finish it, you will have a new set of tools to build trust in any context. You may even re-discover yourself as an agent of connection and change."

Jerome Deroy, CEO, Narativ, Inc.

Dedicated to all past,
present,
and future
Circle Keepers.

"There will be a day [when] the children of all genders,
colors and faiths will follow the path of the heart.
They will speak the language of the earth
and understand the language of heaven.
They will live as part of the great circle of life
and then peace will come."

An Indigenous Prayer
Shared by Tara Brach,
from "How Do We Bridge the Divides?"

Contents

I.

A CIRCLE OF INCLUSION

*If you fall in the
center of a circle,
truth will catch you,
as open hearts
hold the compassion
that lifts you up.*

CHAPTER 1

Finding Connection

Circles provide safe spaces,
releasing the fear
of not knowing,
tapping the wisdom
of what we've known
all along,
finding connection.

I f you feel as though there needs to be change in the world and are seeking a space to make sense of who you are and how you can contribute in a meaningful way, then circles are a useful starting place to develop a stronger sense of self-empowerment. If you're looking for more transparency, communication, and trust in your office, on your team, throughout your organization, or within your community, circles are a tool that can provide the connection that you need. If you want to bring healing, peace, or compassion to discuss issues that are important to you and those around you, regardless of how challenging it is to discuss them, circles offer one of the best solutions available to have those courageous conversations. If you want to create a safe space where there is ample opportunity to see, hear, and value the stories of all backgrounds, views, and cultures, circles are one of the most credible ways to bring about change and welcome everyone's perspective. This book explains the importance of circles and how to use this simple, time-tested tool that is always available to us.

Let's imagine you are in a circle right now.

Welcome. We would open with a purposeful pause to honor you right where you are, realizing that you are a vital part of the circle. Pause now and take a few breaths, breathing longer on the exhalation with your mouth open.

You might be nervous because you do not know what to expect, but your ability to be present without expectation is part of the magic of circles. Perhaps this is your first circle, or maybe you've participated in a circle before. Each circle experience allows you to learn something you've never known before. You will learn about others from their stories, but you will also learn a great deal about yourself. By listening without interruption, truth emerges, trust develops, and a shift in consciousness takes place.

In many respects, a circle is a meditation: a means through which we invite our whole selves, a time at which we slow down long enough to pay attention by listening deeply. When we participate in circles, we share our stories with courage, humility, vulnerability, and transparency. Trust lines the circle container so that it transforms into a safe space to tell the stories that have defined us. In circle, we share our stories, giving them away, because as part of the circle, we realize that we don't own them. Our stories are only the beginning of how we appreciate who we are. We only receive the true depth of wisdom from the gift of our stories when we share them with others.

We come together in circle to give of ourselves, as well as to receive the best of each other. Through this intimate share of our journey, we give each other the courage to dig deeper, to step outside of our comfort zones, and to invite everyone present to share their best and their worst, while both growing and connecting in the process. Underlying the sharing of our stories are the answers we long for and the hope we desire.

Seldom do we experience the world through someone else's eyes, but in circle, we learn to see and acknowledge our own wisdom through the lessons of others. The circle allows the truth to emerge by prompting participants with the right questions. Questions are often more important than answers. You don't have to answer questions in circle. But even your silence speaks volumes. Circles enable us to reflect on questions in a way that we could never do in a facilitated group discussion.

The Circle Way: A Leader in Every Chair, written by Christina Baldwin and Ann Linnea, says that "[s]olid archaeological evidence of hearth rings [or circles] has been excavated in South Africa and dated back 125,000 years." Arguably, circles have been used for thousands of years by Africans, Australians, Native Americans, First Nations, and indigenous people everywhere.

Psychiatrist and philosopher Carl Gustav Jung hypothesized that we share a number of cultural archetypes buried deep in our psyche: the power of circles is one of them. Baldwin and Linnea found that archetypal energy is part of the attraction to the circle process, also viewed as the "magic of circle" that occurs when we come together to listen deeply to one another. In circles, we build community, heal harm, resolve conflict, and form deeper connections and more lasting bonds than the average dialogue, session, forum, meeting, or conversation allows.

We come together
to give of ourselves,
as well as to receive
the best of each other.

There is no posturing in circle. Therefore, circles are better tools for truly listening and understanding one another. As a fact-finding tool for resolving issues, circles are in many respects superior to litigation, arbitration, or mediation because the circle process allows all parties to listen, learn, and understand each other with honesty and trust. If done properly, no blame, shame, or guilt directed to participants is tolerated in circle.

Our circle process is the result of the teachings of many amazing Circle Keepers, including but not limited to Elizabeth Clemants of Hidden Water and Planning Change; Kay Pranis, who wrote *The Little Book of Circle Processes*, the seminal book on circle keeping; and Grandmother Strong Oak Lefebvre who is a Native American master of circle keeping and social justice. Over time, we have continued to work with circles in the diversity, equity (including accessibility and justice), and inclusion (including welcoming and belonging) (together, "belonging and inclusion") space because circles help us all find common ground, build lasting connections, show appreciation, and value one another regardless of our differences.

In circle, we speak from the "I" of our own truth, without ego, lecturing to someone else, or trying to please others. As someone in circle once said, circles are like staring into a mirror of ourselves as we speak from our hearts with compassion. We hold space because we begin by being compassionate for who we are and what we need to say to be present. By sharing our stories, we gather in circle as equals, seeing each other for the first time through open exchanges about challenging issues, painful experiences, or life lessons that have formed and shaped who we are.

In many respects, the pandemic as well as the death of George Floyd allowed circles to emerge in the virtual world by holding more remote circles. Hidden Water held circles for those suffering from childhood sexual abuse on Zoom before the pandemic, but those practices solidified even more during this pivotal time in our history when Zoom and similar software for virtual meetings suddenly became the norm.

Our ancestors who created circles did not likely contemplate that circles would be held through virtual settings made of electronic wavelengths that included images and audio of our shares, similar to how we sat in a circle around the fire.

In a virtual space, circles are created from the repetitive pattern of our shares: we pass a virtual talking piece in the same order, which is put in the chat. On Zoom, you can configure the Zoom boxes to match the order of the chat. Virtual circles do not prevent us from doing circles in person, and in fact, virtual circles increase the likelihood that we hold circles.

Restorative circles are used in schools, in prison systems as part of restorative justice programs, in courts, in cities known as restorative cities, and for a variety of opportunities where we need to connect. Circles have also been used by media companies, first responders, post offices, law firms and departments, Mayor's Offices, and other places of employment.

Although storytelling is the heart of circles, one of the most important aspects of being in circle is not talking but listening. When we are in circle, for the most part, we are holding space for the shares of others. We are engaged in deep listening. One of the most critical aspects of circles and their power to bring about meaningful connection is not what we say, but what we hear. Thus, a critical component of circles is the humility of honoring stories in addition to our own.

Experienced Circle Keepers share that some of the key attributes of circle are to honor the presence and contribution of every person and give an equal voice to all. Confidentiality is also key to ensuring openness and emotional safety. Participation is voluntary; no participant is required to share unless they choose to do so.

The person holding the talking piece introduced by the Circle Keeper is the only one who may speak. The talking piece is passed from person to person, and everyone is expected to respect it. If you are in person, you place the talking piece handed to you in the center of the circle and hold your own talking piece or take one from the center altar to contribute to the conversation. Participants who do not hold the talking piece listen quietly.

A critical aspect of
circles and their power
to make meaningful connections
is not what we say,
but what we hear.

Throughout this book, we invite you to circle with us, and at the end of each chapter, we will provide you with prompts that you can share for a circle round. A "round" represents each time the talking piece is passed around to everyone in the circle.

The first thing that you will need to participate in circle, regardless of whether the circle is in-person or virtual, is a talking piece. Your talking piece can be anything that represents something that is important to you. Your talking piece can be a stone, a crystal, a cap, a toy, a piece of jewelry, a book, clothing, or something that belonged to someone close to you. As long as it's something that can be touched by others, a talking piece can be almost anything.

We say that the power is in the talking piece because the only person who can speak is the one holding the talking piece. We generally begin by introducing ourselves as we pass our talking pieces by sharing a story about the talking piece. For example, Cecilia might hold her favorite talking piece—an amethyst crystal that used to belong to her mother, with a silver angel on top who peers down at a violet stone—and share the following:

> I took this from my mother's possessions after she passed away during the pandemic. She had COVID-19, but she didn't die of it; she died of the loneliness and separation that came with it. At the age of 89, it was more difficult for her to understand why there was no visitation at the hospital during the pandemic. By the time I had convinced the rehab center in St. Claire Shores to put her in the general population so that she could receive visitors, she had already declined to a place from which it was difficult to recover. My mother

surrounded herself with the power of crystals and angels. While her friends focused on more material things when she made her transition, I collected her charms, her scribbled notes for manuscripts that would go unwritten, and her metaphysical books filled with cursive writing that I could identify as hers. The crystal, angel, and their purple hue symbolize the magic that my mother was made of and her ability to trust the unseen. I hold her crystal and its vibrations in my hand, and it becomes my talking piece for circle. In many respects, I have brought my mother to the circle and her ancestors before her. My mother would have loved circle because she enjoyed sharing her truth.

If a circle is remote, the talking piece is passed virtually, but since no one can physically receive it, each participant holds onto their own talking piece. Circles done in person are more focused on the sharing of talking pieces, which are kept on an altar or cloth on the floor in the center of the circle. Each participant introduces their talking piece and hands it to the next person. As each person receives the talking piece, they put it in the center of the circle and then introduce their own. As the circle continues, participants can use one of the talking pieces in the center, which was introduced by someone else. This additional bonding and connecting with talking pieces shared by others is a powerful way to build connection and show respect and compassion for the stories shared in the circle.

How you engage with the talking piece is up to you. We have seen the CEO of an organization use a puppet in a brilliant way, which gave everyone in the circle comfort and joy. We have seen a Fire Captain hold the talking piece with both hands in reverence for the piece itself, showing respect for the circle process and a willingness to engage. Regardless of how we interact with the talking piece, we say that there is "power" in it because only the person holding the talking piece can speak.

Once Cecilia finishes sharing, she passes the talking piece on to Gina. Gina might use Cecilia's talking piece if they are in person or place it in the center of the altar and use one of Gina's favorite talking pieces, a small bottle filled with paper origami stars given to her by her students. Gina would share:

> My students in China gave me this bottle filled with paper stars as a farewell gift when I was leaving China to return home to the U.S. These origami stars represent "lucky stars" or "wishing stars." According to a Japanese legend, the stars are intended to bring the person who made them good luck and provide even more luck when giving them away to a loved one. When I lived in China for two years teaching English, I felt lucky to have students who helped me feel at home. They would all cheerily say "hello" to me as soon as they walked into

the classroom, help translate anything I did not understand from Mandarin Chinese to English and ask me many questions about my life back in the U.S. Whenever I look at this bottle of stars, of which they took the time to fold, I think of their kindness, hospitality, and generosity. By using this as my talking piece, I bring their warmth, compassion, and empathy into the circle to help heal whatever the circle needs.

This new way of holding the talking piece is really very old. It draws on the ancient Native American tradition of using a talking stick passed from person to person in circle, which grants the holder sole permission to speak. It combines this ancient tradition with contemporary concepts of democracy and inclusivity in a complex, multicultural society.

Simply by this expression of deference to listen to the truth of another, we can provide immediate support for all, which is especially important in situations when we need to process current events and interactions; when team responses are needed to address needs in real time; when time-sensitive tools are necessary to build connection, communication, and compassion—whether in schools, workplaces, communities, prisons, governments, or other environments where it would be beneficial to see, hear, and value one another.

The essential rules for circles, shared by the Circle Keeper, are as follows:

Everyone is equal. No person is more important than anyone else.

There is a Circle Keeper, but the keeper participates in the circle and merely guides the process.

Emotional aspects of individual experiences are welcome.

For virtual circles, the order of participation is put in the group chat, but the chat is not used by participants except to note the entries by the circle keepers (*e.g.*, the circle order or the prompt/question) or administrative emergencies (*e.g.*, when someone is not audible or has to depart early).

All participants should be visible via video camera unless they are having technical difficulties. This ensures that participants can see everyone who is present in the circle and that there are no unacknowledged visitors.

The "keeper" leads the circle by making introductory comments and poses the questions ("prompts") to guide the discussion. As mentioned, the keepers are full participants. Generally, one or two keepers can be used. More keepers can be designated to hold space for healing in circles dealing with volatile issues, which guarantees the presence of more people who have the focus and strength to be present for whatever comes up. A talking piece is introduced by the keeper and passed with a hand motion. Keepers should select talking pieces in advance. No one is permitted to watch circles as a spectator since the process is sacred because participants are sharing their truth.

The only person authorized to speak is the person holding the talking piece (one person at a time) moving in one direction.

Participants may pass and choose not to speak during a round and later share in a subsequent round of questions.

When a person is finished speaking, they pass the talking piece to the next person. In virtual circles, the participants may display the motion of passing the talking piece up to the camera and say, "I now pass my talking piece onto [next person's name]."

There can be one keeper or several. Sometimes, there are many keepers within a circle, and in a sense, everyone can perform some or all aspects of the role of Circle Keeper.

More keepers can be designated to hold space for healing in potentially difficult circles.

Crosstalk, speaking out of turn, or even putting something in the chat to comment on what someone shared is prohibited, both during in-person and virtual circles. Passing the talking piece around the circle should allow everyone a chance to share what comes up for them in response to the prompt and/or what others have shared. The circle rules, which may differ according to the type of circle, have helped preserve the sanctity of the circle for years. All participants must only speak from their own perspectives, or as we say, speak from the "I."

The basic rules include the following:

"Respect the talking piece" (everyone listens and has a turn to speak);

"Speak from the heart" (your truth, your perspectives, your experiences);

"Listen deeply" (be patient. Your truth is also revealed through other shares);

"Trust that you will know what to say" (no need to rehearse mentally); and

"Don't ramble" (be concise and considerate of the time for others).

Challenging topics are powerful catalysts for circles because all participants can share their views without judgment. Other participants must listen without interruption and cannot attack or argue with the person holding the piece. Speaking from one's own experience is paramount.

Our experience with circles addressing challenging issues has been positive. The safe spaces that circles provide are an important step towards building the connection and shared feeling of psychological safety necessary for a diverse and inclusive environment where others feel as though they are welcomed and belong. We will later do a deeper dive into the various components of psychological safety and why circles help support it.

As keepers introduce prompts, they may start with a prompt that invites everyone to be more present. One prompt we often use is, "What do you need to say to be present?" If you would like to focus on the topic at issue instead, the first prompt might invite everyone to share an experience that is relevant. In *The Circle Way*, Baldwin and Linnea say that questions are "like a flower that beckons to the bee, and the responses pollinate the ensuing conversation. The question can be designed to strengthen a sense of commonality or to release assumptions that may be preventing the group from considering options and seeing creative possibilities" like perceiving a challenge with hope rather than disenchantment. Some suggested prompts are "How has this situation allowed you to bring out your best?" or "If you could create a new story from this challenge, what would it be?"

If the circle topic is on building community, the first prompt could be "What communities do you belong to?" The second and/or third prompts can be more thought-provoking and probe the topic more deeply. Some examples of these prompts could be "What hinders us from building community?" or "What is a community you want to help build and why?" The last prompt should be one that is positive, healing, and uplifting. An example of a last prompt could be "What is one thing you can do daily to build community?"

Circle Keepers should ensure that everyone takes responsibility for making the circle a welcome, safe place for open dialogue. Keepers can emphasize that "we all have something to learn from each other." Part of ensuring circles are a safe place for dialogue is ensuring that the definition of crosstalk is shared as part of the guidelines so participants can refrain from it. However, participants can reference a share by saying, "When you brought up X, it brought up Y for me," which is not considered crosstalk.

The safe spaces that circles provide
are an important step towards
building the connection and shared
feeling of psychological safety
necessary for a diverse and inclusive
environment where others feel
as though they are welcomed
and belong.

Participants should refrain from directing their shares to other people in the circle, and instead focus on the entire circle. There should be no comparisons, and caution should be exercised to refrain from being judgmental. Wisdom from the circle can be shared, but not the specifics of what someone said. No one should discuss shares outside of the circle. What is said in the circle stays in the circle. Confidentiality means that things that come up in the circle should never be repeated outside of the circle, even if it is two participants communicating with one another. There is no question that the information shared in circle should not be the subject of gossip. The sanctity of the circle is dependent upon its confidentiality. Ideas, rather than the stories themselves, can be shared.

Circle openings are part of the cohesiveness of the circle experience. How we welcome someone to circle greatly impacts their experience. Circle openings build the foundation for trust. Openings eventually align with circle closings like bridges of the connective tissue we need to open our awareness as well as revitalize our strength, emphasizing the power and purpose of the circle with prayer, meditation, affirmation, poetry, quotes, or even a video clip, honoring all that will or has taken place in circle.

When circles open communication channels, resolve conflict, encourage trust, and create a safe space for courageous conversations, they're also cultivating a stronger sense of belonging and are therefore supporting a need that is "hardwired into our biology." As Owen Eastwood teaches in *Belonging: The Ancient Code of Togetherness*, oxytocin, serotonin, dopamine, and endorphins provide collective magic when we feel a sense of belonging. When we feel as though we belong, stress hormones are in balance; anxiety and fear are lowered. We also "trust, communicate, and cooperate at a higher level." We're more empathetic and compassionate. He says, "Endorphins signal moments of social bonding."

The testimonials we have collected about circles in the workplace support this collective magic: they help us become better listeners, elevate our understanding of empathy, teach us patience, help us appreciate different viewpoints, and honor the perspectives of others. Storytelling in any context connects the teller to the hearer in such a powerful way that hearers are transformed from passive bystanders into active participants.

Storytelling is a relational form of communication—the relating of a story literally builds the connection of our relatability. In his book, *Healing the Mind through the Power of Story: The Promise of Narrative Psychiatry*, Dr. Lewis Mehl-Madrona says that "[e]verything is a story, including our identities, ourselves, our meanings and purposes, our theories about the world." He says that our "[b]rains are organs of story, changing to match the needs of their environment, and specialized to understand story, store story, recall story, and tell story."

According to Dr. Mehl-Madrona, we are made up of our stories, and our cultures consist of "all the stories ever told and remembered." *Healing the Mind through the Power of Story* reveals how stories hold "the richness of the interconnectedness and complexity of the world in a way we could never articulate otherwise." Presentations that consist entirely of facts and figures will be swiftly forgotten; presentations that contain stories will not.

In *Belonging*, Eastwood shares that when he was twelve, he wrote a letter to the office of Ngāi Tahu, his family's Māori tribe, and asked them, in essence, "What do you know about who I am?" He didn't expect a reply, but the office replied, saying, "You belong." He was then provided with documentation of his Māori genealogy, going back over 20 generations, referred to as his "*whakapapa*." Eastwood describes *whakapapa* as something that we all have, regardless of tribe. We see it as the connective tissue of humanity, all born from a single tribe, that daily attempts to "belong." He says, "Each of us is part of an unbreakable chain of people going back and forward in time. Back to our first ancestor at the beginning of time and into the future to the end of time. Each of us in this chain of people has our arms interlocked with those on either side of us. We are unbreakable. Together, immortal."

Circles give us an opportunity to find the whakapapa that is missing. The focus in circles starts within so that we strengthen our capacity to honor others by first honoring ourselves, body, mind, and spirit. Like whakapapa, circles build strong teams and a more cohesive community because they "connect us to something greater than ourselves." As Christina Baldwin says in *Calling the Circle*, "[T]he circle [is] a container for human and spiritual energies…[T]here must be an opening in ourselves [which] creates receptivity: brings in insight, interconnection, intuition, and even a sense of spiritual inspiration," and "provides healing potential a place to reside."

How would you open a circle? What important story would you have to share? What talking piece would you bring on this journey through circle with us? No matter what, come without expectation. This journey of change will reveal its own magic.

Welcome to our circle of change.

Our first set of prompts are:

What brought you to the circle?

What change would you like to see take place
in the world?

How can you support those around you?

CHAPTER 2

Remaining Open

*Circles step gently
into vulnerability,
healing old wounds
with the balm
of deep listening,
holding the hearts
of talking pieces,
remaining open.*

Circles begin long before they start. As you join the circle, keep in mind that your self-care is important, especially if you are a Circle Keeper. What you will get out of circle will depend on what you bring to it. So, it is important to bring a growth mindset, which is an open mind, as well as an open heart to whatever comes up. When we train new keepers, we teach that one of the most important aspects of preparation is meditation, prayer, exercise, sleep, and any other well-being practices that support their resilience. The more centered you are, the more in tune you will be to speaking from the heart of your experience, as well as holding space for the stories of others. Once you are in circle, you should be as fully present as possible—both for yourself and for your fellow participants. Peacemaking Circle expert Kay Pranis says that self-preparation is a "core responsibility" of circle.

Self-preparation includes self-care. In *Real Change*, Sharon Salzberg shares that "Self-care is not simply about me time. It can have a lot to do with a sense of fraternity and sisterhood because we're actually replenished and nourished by fellowship. It's enlivened by being in community with others, being able to offer something worthwhile to others." When we come together with tools like circles, we continue to strengthen our self-care and build community that simultaneously supports our resilience.

In *Healing the Mind Through the Power of Story*, Dr. Mehl-Madrona advocates that everyone form a healing circle (*hocokah* in Lakota) to help each other. Although circles were traditionally led by elders, we recognize that there is valuable wisdom in all ages, generations, and cultures. For those of us born in cultures that still maintain some communal traditions of dance, song, trance, tongues, pipes, sweat lodges, and other ways to connect with the power within, centering remains an important ritual. Realizing our oneness with plants, animals, and each other, liberates us from the hectic pace of the world and forces us to listen to the silence.

When we listen in silence, every part of us hears. We hear the inner guidance that is always informing us. When we slow down and listen, we build resilience beyond the ever-changing landscape of politics, war, and self-destruction. Science establishes that meditation actually supports inclusion because it helps calm the mind, makes us less judgmental, and even reduces implicit bias.

The good thing about mindfulness is that it can be talked about in the workplace as non-religious. It offers a secular practice that affords us the ability to be silent together without bias towards or against a particular faith. No one owns the stillness. Stillness invites all of us to center daily and breathe awareness, connection, and trust.

In *The Power of Inclusion*, Cecilia shares her experience with meditation:

> Since I began meditating as part of my spiritual practice around 1974, meditation remains an essential part of my faith. We, however, can remove religious references from meditation so that the practices are more welcoming to those who do not share religious beliefs. Meditation is important in maintaining focus, providing one of the best tools for resilience, and enhancing compassion, kindness, and appreciation.

Mindfulness is one form of meditation, defined as being aware of the present moment without judgment, but we don't limit mindfulness to a particular definition. We like the broad definition of mindfulness that Sharon Salzberg provides and its depth for release and openness. She says, "Mindfulness is the practice of paying attention in a way that creates space for insight."

Meditation is not a religion, but we can choose to incorporate it into every aspect of our lives: our health and well-being, our family and personal relationships, our work and career development, our worldview and community, and our religion and faith. I incorporate meditation in everything that I do, as Brother Lawrence and Thích Nhât Hanh would say, practicing the presence. For example, every Saturday morning, at 7:00 A.M., I hold a circle of prayer. The circle originated from a 40-day prayer circle I held after Easter 2014 to pay tribute to the power of the resurrection of Jesus. We always focus on the crucifixion, but rarely do we consider the teachings that Jesus imparted the 40 days before the ascension.

Our prayers intensified during the pandemic, when we finished 100 consecutive days of prayer, as shared in my book *Good Medicine: 100 Prayers From the Pandemic.* We continue to come together to pray every Saturday in whatever form or shape our prayers take: words, thoughts, silence, presence, awareness, a circle embodying love, as well as mindfulness meditation practices. Our prayer circle creates a space for insight. As our prayer practice deepens, we become aware that the gathering itself is our meditation. We are guided through meditation rather than asking for things. In the breath of a single moment, we realize that we don't have to beg because our miracles are here. The pure presence and power of perfect health and wholeness are always present.

When we are open to an awareness of love expressed as us, we find an altar right in our souls. We can listen to our own breath and be restored. Listening to the breath and being one with the moment is not merely resilience; it is grace.

Meditation is called a practice because we must practice it, and only through practice do we achieve results. We can begin by spending at least a few minutes a day in meditation. When we learn to settle our bodies and practice wise and compassionate self-care, our focus is not on reducing stress but increasing our ability to manage stress, as well as creating more room for our nervous system to find coherence and flow. For example, we can focus our attention on the center of our bellies, behind our navels.

If it is available to you at this very moment, breathe in and out, deeply and slowly, a few times. Breathing in lets us pull the air all the way down into our bellies and then breathe out, releasing all the air through our noses. Let us follow our breath as it flows through our noses, throats, lungs, and then bellies. Keep following it as it flows back out again.

Just meditating 15-30 minutes a day may help reverse the appearance of aging, improve our overall demeanor, as well as reduce our unconscious biases. It does not matter if we are introduced to mindfulness at the mosque, temple, church, dojo, revival, or on the job. The most important thing to do is practice it, and from that starting place, we eventually discover what works best for us. There are ample meditation apps, including, but not limited to, Journey Meditation; Stop, Breathe, and Think; Headspace; Calm; and Cecilia's own daily Mindfulness Blog, at mindfulnessgroup.blog.

We can listen to our own breath
and be restored.

The onus to practice meditation consistently and to develop greater compassion is not the responsibility of some rather than others but what we all should do to tap the power within. Those who have been oppressed in this country have long used the tools of meditation, prayer, devotionals, compassion, gratitude, singing, humming, shouting, and other practices to deal with the trauma of coping with racism and prejudice. Otherwise, we would not have survived the intense brutality of slavery and other forms of genocide, internment camps, Jim Crow, lynching, attacks because of cultural or lifestyle differences, police violence, and other forms of oppression. Practicing meditation does not make us less effective but more resilient in combatting injustice, strengthening ourselves to not only be courageous but to connect with a source greater than our physical experiences. Meditation is as free as the air we breathe and is always available to us.

Meditation is important for circle preparation because it helps reduce implicit bias. The science establishes that we are all biased. No matter how positive we are, we all have a negativity bias. Lawyers, for example, suffer a great amount of internal negativity. Dr. Larry Richard, an expert on the psychology of lawyers and owner of a consulting group called LawyerBrain, says lawyers compound negativity because they are trained to be skeptical, always anticipate what could go wrong, and are hired to be adversarial. Lawyers tend to suffer from high stress and low resilience and have a fixed rather than a growth mindset.

We all embody the historical trauma of our ancestors, who had internal alarms to respond to and protect themselves from physical danger. Our history, experiences, family, education, environments, media, and many other elements also compound our internal alarms with the toxins of shame, blame, and guilt. Just as much as we are biased against others, we are also biased against ourselves.

◉◉◉◉◉◉◉◉◉◉◉◉◉◉◉◉◉◉

Meditation is important for circle preparation because it helps reduce implicit bias.

◉◉◉◉◉◉◉◉◉◉◉◉◉◉◉◉◉◉

To compound our challenge further, our work environments are complex webs of social systems experienced by our brains as stressful, triggering the same defenses required in the harsh terrain thousands of years ago when surviving the attack of animals and the elements as hunter-gatherers. Therefore, we must recalibrate our internal alarm system to manage our inner trauma and create an inclusive mindset that is more positive than negative.

We measure biases through mechanisms like the Implicit Association Test (the "IAT") developed by Mahzarin Banaji and Anthony Greenwald. IAT data reveals that implicit bias is pervasive and approximately 75 percent of Americans display an implicit (automatic) preference for White people over Black people. Similarly, in *Caste: The Origins of Our Discontents*, Isabel

Wilkerson shares that Harvard sociologist David R. Williams found that "80 percent of white Americans hold unconscious bias against black Americans, bias so automatic that it kicks in before a person can process it." Banaji and Greenwald establish that most discrimination against Black people is not explicit, overt prejudice but is implicit and is the primary contributor to the disadvantages experienced by Black people. The toxins of bias run so deep that we cannot reduce them unless we change our consciousness. One way to help reduce implicit bias for all of us is with meditation.

Several studies support the use of mindfulness to reduce implicit bias (*e.g.*, Yoona Kang, Jeremy Gray, and John Dovidio (2013) (the "Kang Study"); Adam Lueke and Bryan Gibson (2014 and 2015) (the "Leuke/Gibson Studies"); and Alexander Stell and the University of Sussex (2015) (the "Stell Study"). In Kang's study, volunteers were assigned to one of three groups to measure their implicit bias against Black people and homeless people. One group practiced a lovingkindness meditation for six weeks; a second group discussed lovingkindness meditations without practicing them; and a third group did not practice any meditations. At the end of the six weeks, the only group whose "implicit bias" against Black people and homeless people "significantly decreased" was the group who practiced the lovingkindness meditation. Just learning, thinking about, and discussing compassion and equality was not enough to change deep-rooted biases.

In the Stell Study, scientists found that participants who performed a seven-minute lovingkindness meditation practice with

Black people as their focal point significantly diminished their bias against Black people.

The Leuke/Gibson Studies showed that meditation in reducing bias does not need to be restricted to lovingkindness meditations.

Participants in both studies engaged in 10 minutes of mindfulness meditation, which showed significantly less bias.

Mindfulness supports circles because it helps us slow down and listen to one another with courage, insight, and compassion, free of judgment.

If we stop, take a moment, and pause to listen, not only are we more aware of our own thoughts and more intuitive to the situations around us, but we also learn to be less judgmental, less critical, and even less biased toward others. Our ability to hold space for one another is enhanced when we are fully present in the moment. When we focus on the inhalation and exhalation of each breath, we are better able to release our worries about the past and the future—and breathe new possibilities by being present without judgment, especially during circle.

Taking a short walk outside, or as we like to call it, a "nature break," is another way to prepare for circle. According to the American Psychological Association, adults who received the recommended amount of physical activity per week, which is about 2.5 hours of brisk walking, had a 25% lower risk of depression. Those who briskly walked for 75 minutes, half of the recommended amount, per week, had an 18% lowered risk of depression compared to adults who reported no physical activity. Studies have also shown that walking helps to reduce stress, aid in better sleep, improve your mood, reduce loneliness, improve creativity, increase self-esteem and confidence, and freshen your focus. Taking nature walks can push our brains to release endorphins, lightening our moods and boosting positive emotions throughout our bodies. When our bodies and our minds feel more relaxed after a nature walk, we can be more present for ourselves and others during circle.

Journaling is another mindfulness practice that helps us prepare for circle. Taking some time to jot down a few pages of what is coming up in our streams of consciousness helps to clear our minds. Dr. Mehl-Madrona says that writing has "great healing power" and has been seen to result in things like fewer health center visits, improvements in immune systems, fewer absences from work, improved physical health, and even better grade-point averages. The content that you write does not need to be articulate, beautiful, poetic, or make any sense. The most important part of the process is just acknowledging what comes up for you without judgment.

Gina shares more about journaling:

> Journaling has been one of the wellness practices that I always turn to regardless of how I am feeling or whether I know what I want to write. To me, writing in a journal is like participating in a circle. They say that being in circle is like talking to a mirror and when I am journaling, I feel like I am writing to my friend and to myself at the same time. Journaling

allows me to share all that I am processing in my mind to see the world in a clearer way. Sometimes, something I write in my journal comes up through my share during a circle and I can share my story more confidently with others because I already took the preliminary steps to process my experience through journaling. Once I write something down in my journal, I don't cross out or erase any words because I trust that what I wrote is how I am authentically thinking and feeling at that moment and have pure trust in my instincts. Trusting my instincts while journaling enhances my ability to trust my instincts during circle.

Take a pen and paper right now and begin journaling as you journey through this book. What has brought you to this moment? What are you open to learning from these pages? What are your values, purpose, wishes, and dreams? What concerns you the most? What ideas, feelings, or situations do you need to release? Let your thoughts wander until you feel like you are ready to take the pen off the paper. Journaling can be done at any point in the day, to prep for, as well as decompress from circle.

Decompressing after circle is just as important as preparing for circle. All participants in circle are fully present, regardless of whether they are designated the Circle Keepers for that circle or not. Emotions of various intensities result from circle, so recharging afterward is crucial. Otherwise, you don't have sufficient time to process the experience. If possible, don't schedule meetings right after a circle ends. Meditating, walking, journaling, stretching, cooking, and napping are additional ways to decompress.

Remaining open throughout the circle process allows circle participants to better receive the gifts that circles offer, as well as remain open to whatever comes up during circles. Keepers should trust their instincts to change course based on something that occurred before the circle or based on the energy of the circle.

Change in circles may take place immediately or over time. But we know that trying to make a difference or bring about change is an ongoing journey. As Sharon Salzberg says in *Real Change*, "With renewed well-being, we see that trying to make a difference may be a long path, and one that is full of obstacles, but it is a good path."

How will you prepare for circle?

What kind of radical self-care best serves you?

How do you start and end the day
by taking care of you?

What do you do to stay above the fray?

How can you support the self-care of others?

Sharing Stories

Circles ride shoulders
of ancestors,
carrying us 'cross
edges of time,
sharing stories.

The power of circles lies in the stories that we share. Thousands of years ago, all cultures began to record their experiences through stories. We are the only species that can communicate through stories with spoken words. Stories are our source of history, religion, entertainment, celebration, and growth. Griots, many of whom were part of a caste of storytellers who preserved storytelling through marriage, are revered because of their gift of story. In some African traditions, the power of the *nommo*, or the word, is sacred because of the word's ability to capture stories. But the history, beliefs, and folklore of all cultures have been kept alive through the tradition of storytelling.

For example, *griots* originated in the 13th century in the Mande empire of Mali, Africa. For centuries, like thousands of other African cultures, the Mande told and retold the history of the empire, keeping their stories and traditions alive. Australians embrace storytelling as a strong tradition of their culture and community engagement. One of many classic Chinese performing arts of storytelling is known as Pingshu, which is derived from the Mandarin Chinese words Ping, meaning "to discuss," and Shu, meaning "book." In the 15th century Edo Period in Japan, Rakugo, a traditional art of storytelling, celebrated a single storyteller, Rakugoka. All cultures have some form of storytelling.

◉◎◉◎◉◎◉◎◉◎◉◎◉◎◉◎◉◎◉◎◉

The history, beliefs, and folklore of all cultures have been kept alive through the tradition of storytelling.

◉◎◉◎◉◎◉◎◉◎◉◎◉◎◉◎◉◎◉◎◉

Our religions are based on oral stories, eventually inscribed on ancient scrolls. When we learn each other's stories, our stories change. Native Americans teach that the synergy of our combined stories is not merely historical; it is prophetic, teaching us to believe in ourselves and uncover wisdom from all our relations, including animals, plants, and the entire universe. Sharing our stories forms meaningful connections and common ground, creating a healing balm of cohesiveness.

Native American psychiatrist and storytelling expert Dr. Mehl-Madrona says in *Healing the Mind through the Power of Story*, "[w]e are all storytellers." Every so-called fact is "the result of many stories, which define meaning, purpose, identity, goals, values—everything that makes life worth living. Our stories are our greatest teachers, revealing to us how to relate and behave and form a community with others."

It's not hard to imagine that during earlier years, when there were no or even fewer electronics, storytelling was the way families engaged with each other. Now, that there are so many mediums to choose from, like books, newspapers, magazines, theater, film, television, videos, podcasts, audiobooks, blogs, etc., we are all stewards of storytelling. Stories offer the sanctuary of reimagining ourselves: sharing joy in what we now realize was a lesson; surviving challenges that we now know made us strong; finding logic in what once appeared illogical; and devising strategies out of what once seemed hopeless.

Sharing our stories forms meaningful
connections and common ground,
creating a healing balm
of cohesiveness.

Storytelling is in our DNA. The power of the word, the *nommo*, is part of all cultures. Enslaved Africans had to rely on stories through memory, witness, and testimonials because they were prohibited from reading. Stories were also carried through the oral tradition of work songs, field songs, spirituals, gospel, blues, jive-talking, jazz, hip-hop, rap, and spoken word in all shapes and forms. As we listen to the stories shared through generations, we feel their strength, carrying words that need to be heard.

Circles support transparency by allowing all stories to be heard and voices to be celebrated. I can honor what is true for me, while respecting what is true for you—without judgment. As the late novelist Toni Morrison said, "Narrative is radical, creating us at the very moment it is being created. . . . Language is meditation." The language of storytelling works for three types of learners: visual learners appreciate the mental pictures storytelling evokes; auditory learners focus on the words and the storyteller's voice; and kinesthetic learners remember the emotional connections and feelings from stories. Facts are 20 times more likely to be remembered as part of a story.

◎◎◎◎◎◎◎◎◎◎◎◎◎◎◎◎◎◎◎◎◎

Storytelling is in our DNA.
The power of the word,
the *nommo*,
is part of all cultures.

◎◎◎◎◎◎◎◎◎◎◎◎◎◎◎◎◎◎◎◎◎

The vulnerability of truth elicited by our stories brings us closer, makes our teams stronger, and allows us to be more curious, authentic, and open. But being vulnerable does not mean disclosing everything. We can control just how much of our story we want to share in circle. As Brené Brown says, "Vulnerability minus boundaries is not vulnerability." Being compassionate, we are careful of expressing our stories as judgment, shaming others, and instead speak our truth.

⊙⊙⊙⊙⊙⊙⊙⊙⊙⊙⊙⊙⊙⊙⊙⊙⊙⊙⊙⊙⊙

Circles support transparency
by allowing all stories to be heard
and voices to be celebrated.

⊙⊙⊙⊙⊙⊙⊙⊙⊙⊙⊙⊙⊙⊙⊙⊙⊙⊙⊙⊙⊙

Circles raise the question that invokes our stories, "What do you need to speak your truth?" Our levels of comfort will differ, so we hold space for each other for whatever we need to share. Circles enhance our power—not to pry into someone else's truth but to hold space for our own, to learn how to honor our own truth while being respectful of the journeys of others.

One of the critical components of circle for us is that shame, blame, and guilt are not to be used to intimidate or make someone feel less than. In Section II, we will explain further why these emotions do not exist when we weave them into the truth of our story. Circles empower us to release the story that caused us shame and begin to tell a new one.

In *The Power of Inclusion: Meditating with Compassion, Healing with Generosity, Leading with Love*, Cecilia shares how she was taught to share her story as a teenager:

> I was taught to share my story by the late Frances Hamburger, my speech coach at Cass Technical High School in Detroit. Giving speeches on democracy for the *Voice of America*, I learned the value and the humility of sharing from the heart and realized my own story was more meaningful than big words or intellectual quotes. She taught me how to uplift my truth as an inspiration to others and how to weave that truth with the beauty of poetry, cultural pride, and the aspiration of the American dream. Through her constant guidance, I learned that our stories motivate, inspire, teach, and, most importantly, heal.
>
> When I share my story, I show vulnerability, which creates a safe space for others to share. When someone else shares, I embrace their story, and because of the trust we build, my story is no longer my own. I leave it with them, and if something in me needs to be healed, I am closer to healing because releasing my pain

in a safe space offers me an opportunity to
begin again.

We must be courageous enough to let our stories go and not
be afraid to reveal who we are through our truth. In telling our
stories, our job is to give to the audience, not take from them.
Storytelling is also an important teacher, teaching us how to engage with confidence, how to trust our judgment, how to
connect with our audience, and how to be vulnerable with humility.

Circles empower us
to release the story
that caused us shame
and begin to tell
a new one.

Gina was taught to share her story during high school, on-air
at her local Greek radio station, where she participated in youth-
centered discussions around society, education, and future academic and professional ambitions. Although Gina is ethnically
Malaysian Chinese, she learned to speak fluent Greek from her
babysitter in childhood. This experience not only helped her own
the power of her story in a different language to a wider audience

but also demonstrates the common ground that we all share despite our perceived differences.

In circles, our stories are often spontaneous. We believe that we have one thing to share, but as we listen, another story emerges. Grandmother Strong Oak says we should listen so deeply that we have no idea what we will share next. This can be difficult when we think with the ego rather than the heart. But part of the magic of circle is staying open to the stories that it unfolds. Perhaps you anticipate sharing a story about your father, but based on the stories shared by others, you are reminded of a more poignant story about an illness or something that happened at work. What happens through circle is that by leaning into what comes up for us, we establish a foundation of common ground that is restorative.

We should listen so deeply that we have no idea what we will share next.

A story is more than a rehearsed presentation. A story is a tool of transformation that may paint a picture, teach a lesson, save a soul, or even ease a burden. In a circle, we deliver stories in a unique way, often revealing things we have never said before. We discover truths that surprise us because they have never been told, and we hold healing space for souls who must share their truth but cannot bear the telling alone.

Since storytelling is healing, the best techniques for sharing stories are worth learning. Storyhood and Narativ provide some powerful storytelling tools. One of the most important aspects of sharing your story is making sure that you convey it in the most empathetic manner so that it is genuine.

One way to tell a story is through a poem, especially for those things that are too difficult to say directly. Poetry allows us to tell our story indirectly, with heart and meaning that cannot be expressed in prose. In 2020, Cecilia published a book of poetry entitled *Unbroken Circles: Holding Spaces, Finding Forgiveness, Transcending Edges*, which tells a number of stories through poetry that can also be used to open or close circles.

You will learn that some of the people you thought you had nothing in common with are kindred spirits. While doing an exercise led by the NYC Office of Creative Conflict Resolution, participants selected a partner in a group thought to be most different from themselves and exchanged stories about their likes and dislikes. To their surprise, participants had an incredible amount in common with those who looked nothing like them. It was a great lesson in how storytelling helps remove the barriers of perceived differences. Cecilia recalls doing the exercise with a white male Emergency Medical Services officer: "We found that we were more alike than different and enjoyed nearly all the same things."

Our stories are gifts that reveal the common ground we share, the most vulnerable teaching moments, and the values that inform our wisdom. We never know who someone is until we hear their story. Circles are an important catalyst in what we share and how we bless others with our own lasting memories.

We never know who someone is until we hear their story.

"Our memory is best designed to store emotional information communicated through story," according to Dr. Mehl-Madrona. He also teaches that stories are more than a memory; they are a catalyst for change. As Poet Laureate Amanda Gorman shared in her inaugural poem during President Joe Biden and Vice President Kamala Harris's inauguration, with our stories, we have "the power to author a new chapter. To offer hope and laughter to ourselves. So while we once asked, how could we possibly prevail over catastrophe? Now we assert, How could catastrophe possibly prevail over us? We will not march back to what was, but move to what shall be . . . If we merge mercy with might, and might with right, then love becomes our legacy, and change our children's birthright. So let us leave behind a country better than the one we were left with."

In *The Ceremonial Circle*, Sedonia Cahill and Joshua Halpern teach that separation and battles of people against each other and nations against nations are outdated. They say, "We live in a time when it is necessary to weave a new story together." Circles are more than mere containers of words; imbued with the power to change, they are part of the catalyst for telling a new story.

Pause in the power of your story:

Where has your story brought you to this day?

What is the story that best defines who you are?

What stories have you used to heal others?

How can you tell a new story?

What story can you share to support world peace?

CHAPTER 4

Building Community

Circles pose questions,
bridging differences,
establishing common ground,
hearing our own voice
through the ears of others,
building community.

When Rev. Dr. Martin Luther King, Jr. preached a vision of the community called "Beloved," he left it to us to shape and mold its emergence. Listening is one of the most profound ways to build a beloved community and the only way to build a community of compassion. But listening is not easy. Most of us do not take the time to listen because it is so much easier to be consumed by the noise around us. But if we pause to listen, not only are we more aware of our own thoughts and more intuitive to the situation around us, we learn to be less judgmental, less critical, and even less biased toward others.

How can we become better listeners? Circles are truly one of the best ways we've ever experienced how to learn to listen deeply. Preparing for circle through the ways mentioned in Chapter 2, such as meditation, for example, helps us to acknowledge what is keeping us from being able to listen deeply. The prompt, "What do you need to say to be present?" helps circle participants address the things on their minds—work anxiety, micro-aggressions, worry, democracy, children, aging parents, meeting deadlines, getting sufficient sleep, accomplishing goals, hunger, morning commutes, spills, illnesses, death, racism, sexism, nagging inner critics, and so on—so they can try to put their fears and concerns aside and give the circle their undivided attention.

The listening and telling of stories during circle is a reciprocal relationship.

Radical listening requires listening quietly without judgment and giving your full attention to the speaker. We practice radical listening at all times throughout the circle process, allowing each speaker to feel truly heard.

The experience of listening to others' stories is just as important as telling them. The listening and telling of stories during circle is a reciprocal relationship where, as Murray Nossel says in *Powered by Storytelling: Excavate, Craft, and Present Stories to Transform Business Communication*, "listening is the container that gives shape to the telling." When all participants in the circle are radically listening, we feel more courageous to share the most vulnerable parts of our stories. On the other hand, if those in the circle seem distracted and uninterested in listening, then we will not feel comfortable sharing as much, which will affect if and how we tell our stories.

◉◉◉◉◉◉◉◉◉◉◉◉◉◉◉◉◉◉◉

Listening is one of the greatest gifts we can give someone.

◉◉◉◉◉◉◉◉◉◉◉◉◉◉◉◉◉◉◉

Listening is one of the greatest gifts we can give someone. As author Catherine Burns says in *All These Wonders: True Stories About Facing the Unknown*, "[w]e live in a world where bearing witness to a stranger's unfiltered story is an act of tremendous compassion. To listen with an open heart and an open mind and try to understand what it's like to be them . . . takes real courage." Being present for others as they share their story is one of the most important ways to acknowledge that someone else is valuable. Listening is how we show up and give our best without focusing on what we want in return.

Most misunderstandings occur because we fail to listen without judgment. Listening is not a space where we create our own narrative or impose judgment on others. Instead, listening is an opportunity for us to be fully present and curious about the stories of others.

Perhaps you have something painful or difficult to share: I can help you heal that part of your suffering by listening. Maybe you want to tell me something that I'm afraid to hear because I believe that I am to blame for your suffering: listening opens spaciousness that allows me to hold what is important to you and gives both of us the ability to heal. If I don't listen, I am left to my imagination, and we both continue to suffer.

Listening helps us share the words that need to be dislodged from deep in our souls. Listening helps us pull from our consciousness whatever troubles us or even gives us joy. By speaking our words, we release our anxieties, our cares, and our fears. Many of us are afraid to listen to the suffering of others because we may feel like we are guilty of the pain caused. Similarly, we may not want to listen to others who have caused harm because we may feel like they are so oblivious to the pain caused that their ignorance is too difficult to bear. Listening without judgment is the first step towards healing.

When we cannot trust those we share our truth with, we will not have full communication. We will, then, not reveal too much, especially not those things that would make us vulnerable. Radical listening is a sacred contract that simply allows us to hear what is important to someone else without judgment or risk of condemnation, which helps to create a safe space. Radical listening allows us to share our imperfections, our shame, and our vulnerabilities— without worrying that what we share will make us less than or turn into something that can be used against us.

**Listening helps us share the words
that need to be dislodged
from deep in our souls.**

Listening dyads, which are exercises where two people take turns listening to each other, are beneficial. The listening portion is timed: one, two, or three minutes. The period is generally short because listening is difficult to do. We need to gradually increase the timing to press against our impatience and learn to be fully present for each session. That's what we love about circles, which we discuss more fully in the next chapter.

Everyone must be listened to, no matter how long it takes. While you listen to everyone share and pass the talking piece, you realize that sometimes it is not our stories that heal us but the stories of others.

There is a powerful circle that we did when we were being trained as Circle Keepers by an organization called Planning Change. Our circle training was in-person for five days straight at seven hours each day. During one of the training sessions, Elizabeth Clemants, our trainer, took about 15-20 sticks out of a bag and placed them at the altar, which is in the center of the circle. When it was our turn to share, we had to interact with the sticks in any way we chose without speaking. Each person interacted with the sticks in different ways, such as hitting them together, using them to build a structure, and making music. This employed our storytelling and listening skills in a new way, in which we used our heightened senses to observe and interpret what each person was trying to convey through the sticks without words.

What are the different ways you could use sticks to express who you are and what you want to say in circle?

In a circle, you can only speak from your own experience. You can only touch the edges of your own pain and suffering, your own confusion and messiness, or perhaps even your own light and love. You are forced to listen. By the time the talking piece reaches you, you have opened a space within yourself that needed opening—only because you heard someone else's story.

Only through listening do we discover that what is important to someone else is different from what is important to us, or maybe it's the same. We learn that our thoughts are only one aspect of a myriad of differences. We learn that we have a gift to share that requires nothing monetary. We can cultivate spaces of giving and receiving that we never knew we had within us.

When we radically listen to one another during circle, we realize we are more similar than we are different. We realize we are on a common ground that we all share. We get to know all the participants as who they are as human beings, abandoning any preconceived notions we had of them. We become more compassionate and appreciative of everyone in the circle and build stronger bonds as a group. We collaboratively build Rev. Dr. Martin Luther King, Jr.'s vision of a beloved community.

Building community is the foundational step needed in circle before circles about more difficult topics can be discussed. We can build community through circles not only by radically listening, but also by sharing our stories, referring to someone's share without cross talking, opening to and selecting someone's talking piece, and even appreciating a silent share with sticks. This fosters trust that whatever is said in the circle, regardless of how challenging, will be heard with compassion, without judgment.

All circles offer opportunities for deep listening.
We begin by learning about each other
and the wisdom we have to offer each other.
Prompts can be about any subject
that the circle would like to embrace,
like racial inclusion, democracy, psychological safety,
or emotional intelligence.

For example, prompts can be:
What experience taught you about self-awareness?
How do you regulate your triggers?
How do you show empathy?
How do you practice humility?

II.

A CIRCLE OF BELONGING

Circles are a harbor
of connectivity sowing change
with each share:
your story becomes
my own,
and mine becomes yours.

CHAPTER 5

Holding Space

Circles are alchemy to the soul,
strength supporting us
wherever it hurts,
spirit winds liberating us,
harnessing magic,
holding space.

C ecilia heard her mother's words, "Let the circle be unbroken," long before she realized she was a Circle Keeper. Cecilia's mother "Myrtle" was born in Columbia, South Carolina, to a mother who made her transition before Myrtle was four years old. So, Myrtle practically raised herself, going to school even though the aunt who raised her tried to make her stay at home to take care of Myrtle's cousin, the aunt's newborn. Myrtle always felt a calling for wisdom and ended up getting her degree in education and childhood development at the University of Detroit. "Let the circle be unbroken," Myrtle said to Cecilia, often teaching Cecilia about the stories of enslaved Africans whose brutal journey through life was forged from countless rapes, murders, beatings, and other forms of brutality in "an attempt to make us feel less than." For Myrtle, the circle extended beyond the physical as a metaphysical connection with ancestors, like the mother Myrtle never knew. "Let the circle be unbroken," she told Cecilia, meaning we have the strength to remain connected beyond our circumstances and realize a power greater than the racism, hatred, and prejudice perpetuated in a country that profited from the oppression, fear, and marginalization of people of color.

When we look at the ancient circles of stone, it's not hard to imagine that human beings were in tune with the sun, moon, seasons, directions, clouds, and stars beyond mere physical survival and were urged to listen to something bigger than ourselves: a creative consciousness that helped inform decisions, choices, and lives in a way that provided power.

"Let the circle be unbroken."

Cecilia first led circles unknowingly: for her church when they prayed; to share stories during spiritual retreats; and at work for courageous conversations. She appreciated this formation, this shape of both equality and equanimity that our ancestors convened for over a hundred thousand years—that called to her. What happened without her realizing it is that the same container of trust was built to hold the truth of her experience that helped her ancestors rise above the fray and find the source of their own power.

In circle, we return to the source of creative consciousness, which lifts us above the fray of discord to a more unified energy of peace. At various points throughout our lives, the autonomy that we need to survive as individuals through the choices that we make causes us to feel as though we are alone when, in reality, we are very much together, sharing a common ground of challenges that unite us as human beings. This was evident to Gina when she first experienced circles in her fifth-grade class, taught by Mrs. Torres. Every Friday at 3 PM, Mrs. Torres would gather all the students into one large circle for a session called "Group" to share academic challenges, conflicts with one another, and ways to support each other. "Group" provided the space for the students to iron out tensions together, establishing a bond of civility, appreciation, and trust that remains many years later.

We belong to each other. We are here for each other. The connection that we have to each other and to our ancestors for generations is not merely tied to pain and trauma but to the purpose and enlightenment that we share. In the United States, we all came here or at least ended up here for a common purpose, and we are only able to be a blessing to this sacred land by honoring the practices that are sacred to those indigenous to it. In circle, there is no greed, no bullying, no superiority, no domination, only the sacredness of being one people, one tribe, one collective wisdom.

In "The Naming of America: Fragments We've Shored Against Ourselves," Johnathan Cohen writes that the "name AMERICA or AMERRIQUE in the Mayan language means, a country of perpetually strong wind, or the Land of the Wind, and ... the [suffixes] can mean ... a spirit that breathes, life itself." We must heal the ugliness of oppression and the brutality of domination that ironically built a country on principles of liberty and justice for all. The principles of democracy are ideas that are bigger than who we are in the flesh. Democracy is a spirit of compassion for all—as vital as the breath of life itself. There is something in the breath of spirit undergirding this land of the free and the home of the brave that many still immigrate to America to find for themselves, something that stands for what we are striving to give to all. If we are on these "waves of grain, purple mountain majesties, fruited plains, with grace shed on us, in crowned good, in brotherhood from sea to shining sea," it is our responsibility to recapture the spirit of love and support that is not only the foundation of our country but also our hope for the world.

The most long-avoided conversations require us to hold space for healing so that we can listen, process, and change our consciousness by bringing peace to those spaces that must be restored. Circles await us as a starting place for deep listening.

Ultimately, there is no script for what arises in circle. Even when we have chosen the words and decided on a direction, we should remain open to the questions of our hearts that emerge as effortlessly as spirit breathing life itself. When we teach circle, one of the most important exercises is for Circle Keepers to learn to be agile in what the circle informs them to ask. The circle listens, hears, processes, and speaks as a spiritual catalyst of inclusion. When we come together, we are more open to welcoming one another right where we are; we feel a more intimate sense of belonging; and we build a stronger foundation from a shared awareness of the need to hold space for one another. We have led circles without knowing what the prompts will be until we are in tune with what the circle says needs to be resolved.

The most long-avoided conversations
require us to hold space for healing
so that we can listen, process,
and change our consciousness
by bringing peace to those spaces
that must be restored.

The "talking piece" is a catalyst for not only talking but also listening. When Cecilia is venting, her husband Marlon hands her the talking piece—not so that she can talk, but to say slow down and listen to yourself. Similarly, when you are holding the talking piece in circle, you should use it as a catalyst to slow down, re-center, and breathe in the present moment. You are not required to share. In fact, one of the most powerful shares we've observed is when someone just held the talking piece in honor of the person's story shared just before they received the talking piece. The circle is an important witness to the stories of those present, and through our witness, we can build a container of some of the most important stories of our life experiences. We hold the sanctity of uninterrupted truth in circle, and we pass the symbol of that wisdom to one another.

Here, we pause because when you speak, we allow ourselves to hold space for you to share; and together, we liberate pain and suffering. The pain that comes up for us might have been sitting in our bodies and the bodies of our ancestors for decades or centuries: the pain of generations of trauma that came before us, that suffered because of genocide camps or ovens, dehumanizing enslavement, colonization, internment, or other forms of annihilation.

Cecilia remembers being in a racial justice training one weekend in New York City. At the end of the first day, she went home, feeling as though nothing happened, but after dinner, she began to weep because she felt the trauma of racism that she struggled through daily but buried through the years so that she could cope. Circles are like tonglen meditation: strong enough to hold pain and, through that invitation, transform it into deliverance. The pain that we suffer, whether real or imagined, dissipates when it is shared.

Take a moment and think about times in your life when you have held the proverbial talking piece and held space for someone else's story. What effects did that have on you and the other person? At what other points throughout your day can you hold space for someone else? What stories of suffering do you carry that need to be cleansed?

Circles are sacrosanct, almost holy; no one interrupts. No one is required to speak when they receive the talking piece, but everyone is invited to do so. All participants are treated equally, regardless of rank or title. By building a foundation of wisdom based on shared stories, experiences, and perspectives, the circle becomes a strong container—powerful enough to *hold* emotions that are difficult to process. We fight the tears that often fall in circle as pain is released, as closure is achieved, as joy is experienced.

In circles, there are "shifts," which are moments of enlightenment. Sometimes, we "shift" because of what we share. Sometimes, our ability to "hold space" for someone else's story is what we need to discover something about ourselves. Circles not only reveal our own suffering but also how we have harmed others. Sometimes anger enters the circle, which is necessary to express. Anger can be a catalyst to release toxins, move beyond pain, and even open our hearts to forgiveness.

Judge Raymond E. Kramer and his colleagues Sethu Nair, Halley Anolik, and Justo Sanchez were the first people to introduce the power of restorative circles to us. They were part of the Center for Creative Conflict Resolution at OATH (the Office for Administrative Trials and Hearings), which provides NYC agencies with positive, inclusive ways to resolve conflict. The Citywide Roundtable Leadership Council is a vital resource for the leadership of restorative circles. Other significant resources include the Restorative Justice Initiative, Hidden Water, and the Visioning B.E.A.R. Circle Intertribal Coalition led by Strong Oak Lefebvre and others. Grandmother Strong Oak uses "Walking in Balance with All Our Relations" to help train others to use restorative circles.

> Sometimes, our ability
> to "hold space" for someone else's story
> is what we need to
> discover something
> about ourselves.

Hidden Water, led by Elizabeth Clemants, focuses on healing circles for victims of childhood sexual abuse, so there is an intentional journey from harm to healing. The pain, shame, and betrayal of loved ones who could not be trusted, including abusive parents and family friends, must be held, processed, and resolved to address the trauma.

Both those harmed and healed (and we all wear both hats) need a safe space to figure out how to leave the past and tell a new story. Circles help us regain our sense of power and self-esteem. We dig deep for our truth, and we begin to value ourselves in a new way. New York City recognizes the importance of restorative practices by requiring all city agencies to use them. Like Detroit and Oakland, several other cities are considered "restorative cities" because they utilize restorative practices in several of their services, systems, and programs.

By passing the talking piece, we can listen to concerns that we would not otherwise hear. We can offer resources to those we would not otherwise know are in need. We can renew ourselves and regain awareness of our purpose simply through the process of sharing with others. Most importantly, passing the talking piece in circles and honoring whatever needs to be processed builds a strong community of solidarity for whatever needs to be addressed. Circles interwoven in culture and integrated in the workplace can be tapped as necessary to address conflict and heal harm.

Healing circles are based on the indigenous teachings and values of the Tlingit and Tagish people of Canada, who taught circle author and teacher Kay Pranis and authorized her to teach the peacemaking circle process. Both she and Elizabeth Clemants teach restorative circle intensives, *which are one of the most powerful experiences we have ever had.* Not only did we learn technique, but we also experienced the benefits of the circle as participants.

We developed more clarity regarding our relationships with others, deeper insight into how to move forward with our goals, and, most importantly, the weight of several emotional burdens we carried was lifted. Cecilia's training with Grandmother Strong Oak and her team provided a powerful training of indigenous practices that address racial injustice and sexual violence and help heal body, mind, soul, and Spirit with restorative circle practices.

Circles interwoven in culture
and integrated in the workplace
can be tapped as necessary
to address conflict
and heal harm.

Courageous, or what some call "difficult," conversations about race and other demographics in the safety of a circle are important because we live and work in a multicultural society and thus must engage in meaningful racial dialogues with one another. In *Holding Space: A Guide to Mindful Facilitation*, Kate Ebner and Izzy Martens say, "The goal of [circles] is to hold space in a way that creates impact, stirs up emotion and ultimately creates positive change." Similarly, we prefer to call these conversations "courageous," which points to their ability to magnify rather than minimize our strength.

Dr. Derald Wing Sue, the author of *Race Talk and the Conspiracy of Silence*, says encountering "diverse racial points of view, being able to engage in racial conversations, and successfully acknowledging and integrating different perspectives leads to an expansion of critical consciousness." Sharing our individual stories engages the cross-racial interactions and dialogue necessary to increase racial literacy and dispel misinformation. Circles are best practices for the strong containers that can hold space for healing our lives amidst the deep-seated racism, sexism, heterosexism, ageism, ableism, classism, antisemitism, and other forms of hatred tearing our country apart.

Here are prompts to consider for circle
or just to respond to in your journal:

How have you harmed others in the past,
and how have you been harmed?

What can we do to support one another?

What are some of your greatest lessons?

What have you experienced that resulted in change?

CHAPTER 6

Creating Trust

Circle stories
are like trees —
roots digging deep,
limbs extending,
welcoming,
touching,
holding branches,
creating trust.

C ircles are one of the most powerful vehicles to tell our stories because they create trust by fostering safe spaces where everything is supposed to remain in confidence, without judgment. In confidence, without judgment, we can share without fear of reprisal or ridicule. We can share our mistakes, inviting others to share similar mistakes, solidifying oneness through vulnerability, thereby creating trust. As peace activist and Buddhist teacher Stephen Fulder shares in conversation with Tara Brach: "Trust supports our ability to stand steady. Trust says, 'I can meet what next arises.'"

In circle, we meet what next arises by sharing that is patient, nurturing, and caring. Circle requires us to follow a certain decorum of respect. You must follow the circle rules. You must speak only from the "I." Circle invites us to correct ourselves. Are you able to pause long enough in the silence to share only when you hold the talking piece? Do you insist on crosstalk, so that you can make a point? Following circle rules helps build our character and competence to be fully present for others, which is not merely for us to share but to realize the importance of the stories of others. When we communicate with reverence and respect in accordance with the circle rules, our connections increase and our trust grows deeper roots.

As we create more trust, we establish a ritual of how we share and show up for one another. Even one circle can cultivate an environment of trust, but the more frequently we circle together the more powerful the engagement.

The key components of trust that develop through circle are Compassion, Agility, Respect, and Education, which stand for C-A-R-E. The CARE framework is set forth as follows.

C – Compassion

When we receive the talking piece, it is important to speak from the heart of our own experiences and be compassionate to ourselves and whatever may come up for us to share in that moment. We also listen with compassion by expressing care for others. We listen with care. We pay close attention to pronouns. We arrive with openness and receptivity, mirroring others' emotions to help them feel less alone.

We do the work that needs to be done before circle by taking care of ourselves. We meditate. We pray. We nap. We release. We cleanse. We show up with strength and capacity to give more grace and light in case someone else is unable to do so in the moment. The energy of care from even a few people cultivates a synergy of goodwill that is infectious throughout the circle.

In *Real Change*, Sharon Salzberg teaches us that compassion is one of the most important attributes of cultivating change. Compassion "implies boundaries (movement toward, not into); balance (compassion for all, including ourselves); stability rather than shakiness; and clarity rather than overidentification." Compassion is one of the most vital forms of well-being as "it helps us avoid burnout and fatigue by teaching us how to say no when we need to, without guilt, and learning to build boundaries. . . Saying no is a courageous act and can be empowering."

When we approach ourselves and each other with compassion, we have less of a tendency to perceive the challenges that we are bound to encounter as a threat.

A – Agility

Circles require the resourcefulness of agility. The more we do circles, the more we develop the capacity to be present to what's there and to pivot from what we thought was important. Sometimes we don't use the prompts we planned and are guided by our intuition instead. Circle Keepers should be agile so that they are in tune to the energy of the circle, so if they feel compelled to share a different opening, prompt, or closing than what they originally planned to share, it's not only acceptable, it's preferable.

Cecilia believes in training keepers to make up prompts in the moment so that they are not reliant on scripts but are genuinely in tune to what comes up in the circle. One of the gifts of being trained as a minister is the spontaneity of prayer and meditation. While at the Fire Department of New York, Cecilia would often be asked to fill in as a Chaplain—only seconds before the Invocation or Benediction was to take place. This is the sort of agility required of a Circle Keeper.

She remembers when she was asked to lead a circle for an office at FDNY because they had been experiencing a great deal of conflict. The Chief who invited her did not describe what the conflict was or who it was between. However, after a few hours in circle with the entire office, trusting what came up for her, the conflict was identified and resolved by the circle participants. Part of the agility required was the use of prompts that went to the heart of the dispute. Because Cecilia was open and listening to what was being shared, she was able to devise the right prompts to respond to the issues that needed to be resolved.

It is important to note that asking the right questions requires foundational work—starting with the easy, community-building prompts, and establishing common ground—before you put questions in the circle that go to the heart of a dispute. This is why it is good to start with circles to build community before using them for disputes. Creating a culture of circles establishes them as a powerful tool that is always at your disposal regardless of the topic.

We must be in tune with what is spoken and what is apparent from how we feel. Agility requires us to be present through every aspect of our being, including our body language. Agility requires a generous, giving spirit, which may encourage a smile, a nod, or even silence when you receive the talking piece. You may need to pause and just lift up someone's previous share. Agility requires that we be fully present for all shares: the easy shares and the challenging ones; those shares you can relate to because you have a similar background or experience, as well as those you can't. Part of being agile is identifying commonalities with circle participants so that we are vocal about sharing common ground. This fluidity provides an energy of celebration and joy, allowing our stories to unfold more easily. Through the agility of common shares, the pattern of similarity is woven into a tapestry of meaningful connections that support a continued rapport: *I trust you because we share a common experience.*

R – Respect

Respect is part of the chemistry of circle. The energy of silence itself, showing that we are attentive and focused on what is being shared shows respect. Dignity, empathy, and transparency contribute to respect, which is a moral compass governing what we share. *I may not have the courage to talk about my father's mental illness, but because you shared your story about your father, I am able to share my truth through my respect for you. Yet, I can also share whatever I wish.* Boundaries are respected; there is no obligation to share anything other than what you desire.

We respect what comes up for others. We respect our ability to be willing vessels to convey the truth that needs to be heard. Participants also show respect to others in the circle by keeping the session time in mind during their shares, ensuring that there is enough time for everyone to have an opportunity to share. When we genuinely care for others to be able to share their experience and respect the equanimity of the flow, we sacrifice our time so that others can be heard. Even if we may disagree or feel discontent over what someone else shares, we respect their ability to be different.

In her book *Calling the Circle: The First and Future Culture*, Christina Baldwin says that respect is also "an important part of how we open and close circle." Openings lay the foundation for what enters the circle. If it is compassion, a lovingkindness or *metta* meditation should be used. If it is healing, perhaps a prayer can be used. If it is a peace circle, stories of peace can be used. Closing a circle requires equal respect for its purpose. We can ask what we hope to take from the circle and what we hope to leave behind. We experience circle with intensity, and afterward, with respect, we release the experience and move on.

E – Education

In circle, we educate each other by listening to understand rather than to respond because we are not talking directly to circle participants. Talking to someone else through our response, as opposed to sharing our insights, would be akin to cross talking. Circles are not meant to be used as a soapbox or to give a speech to anyone in circle. Directly responding to what someone else shares would be breaking the rules of no cross talking and not speaking from the "I." When we listen to understand, we are educated by the shares of others. When we are open and receptive, without judgment, we grow in awareness. New participants to circle breathe a sigh of relief when they realize they are not under attack but there is a mutual give and take of experiences. When we hold the talking piece to share our truth, we educate others about ourselves through our stories. In circle, we say, "Listen to know and share to be known," which helps establish trust.

Circles create healing spaces of welcoming, belonging, and valuing through verbal and nonverbal communication. We say that circles are the gift that keeps giving because they not only give to us but also to others. Almost in the same way that hands are sometimes held in circles, in restorative or healing circles, hearts are held as we create an atmosphere of deliberate truth-telling by centering on all that brings us to the moment. Each share drops the proverbial mic and pours a healing balm of truth that is cleansing simply because it is honest.

Circle Keepers are a combination of teachers, facilitators, leaders, and ministers, as well as participants. They help cultivate trust by maintaining the circle rules, interjecting silence and recentering the group process.

Cecilia has been in healing circles for those who suffered sexual abuse as children and witnessed healings take place because of the deep faith and conviction of the keepers. There is a difference between religion and faith. The religious diversity of circles may not be tolerant of traditional religious expression, but the catalyst of faith in the power of the unseen and the healing energy of love does impact circle. Keepers can build trust by sending an energy of lovingkindness to all participants.

During in-person circles, trust can also be established by our use of the talking pieces that are shared by the circle and how they are placed in the center. We pick up participants' pieces with reverence, respect, and compassion for who they are. For a moment, we are their witness, feeling the energy from whatever inanimate object they held as a talking piece and shared through their stories.

Circles provide the "psychological safety" of which trust is a key component. Psychological safety, which is discussed in the last chapter as well, is a phrase that is used often in the belonging and inclusion space. Positive, supportive, and real communication is pivotal to creating an environment that allows humans to thrive. According to psychologist Dr. Abraham Maslow, who developed the well-known "Hierarchy of Needs," humans need a minimum of their basic needs met (*e.g.*, food, shelter, water) to survive and become more motivated to achieve higher-level needs, such as self-actualization. According to a 2023 McKinsey & Co. article, "Social scientists now believe that psychological safety is one of these basic needs, a prerequisite for people to be at their best in all aspects of life, including home, school, and work."

What is psychological safety? Dr. Amy C. Edmondson, who coined the term, said that a workplace with psychological safety is one where people feel like they can speak up, propose ideas, and ask questions without fear of punishment or embarrassment. According to one McKinsey survey, an overwhelming 89% of employee respondents said they believe that psychological safety in the workplace is essential. Beyond establishing an atmosphere of "belonging" at work and fostering a more diverse and inclusive work environment, psychological safety is necessary for the innovation achieved by successful teams. In 2014, Google studied 180 of its teams as part of "Project Aristotle" and found that brilliance and resources do not compensate for what a team may lack in psychological safety. Psychological safety was the most important factor explaining high performance.

Circles foster psychological safety by providing a space in which everyone is included, is encouraged to learn from one another, and contributes and shares their own perspectives without judgment.

Circles foster psychological safety by providing a space in which everyone is included, is encouraged to learn from one another, and contributes and shares their own perspectives without judgment. Without psychological safety, people operate on fear—fear of introducing new ideas, innovating solutions, and taking risks.

Dr. Timothy Clark, author of *The 4 Stages of Psychological Safety*, defined psychological safety as a condition in which you feel included, safe to learn, safe to contribute, and safe to challenge the *status quo*—without fear of being embarrassed, marginalized, or punished. Learner safety is especially important to building trust in circle because we are all constantly learning about ourselves, each other, and the world around us in circle. The most vulnerable parts of us—especially stories around shame, blame, and guilt—can arise during circle, which provides a safe space to process those emotions because they are containers of trust. We need to be in an environment that supports trust to heal.

Those who feel safe to learn have more capacity to reflect on their performance, take risks, and be more courageous when taking on new challenges. In circle, participants who feel safe to learn might share something that they have never shared aloud in front of anyone else before, initiating the extension of trust to see if that trust will be reciprocated. Learner safety doesn't happen unless it is modeled, communicated, taught, measured, recognized, and rewarded. Gratefully, with the circle rules, the circle process inherently builds an atmosphere where learner safety is supported.

Gina shares that as a Chinese American, she thinks of trust as building "guanxi," loosely translated in Chinese society as personal connections, relationships, or social networks. As someone who lived in China for two years as a U.S. Peace Corps Volunteer, she learned that she needed to develop trust, or guanxi, with her host family, students that she taught, colleagues, and fellow Peace Corps Volunteers to be successful. Building guanxi requires getting to know, spending time with, and helping your community. Building guanxi is critical in both personal and professional contexts in China. Similarly, building trust is critical in circle.

In spaces outside of circle, where cross talking is more frequent, individuals may feel less comfortable sharing their stories. They may be interrupted while sharing their experiences, as well as hear reactions filled with judgment. The good news is that the more we practice circle, the more we bring the foundations of circle to our interactions outside of circle. This is why the more we learn the foundations of a circle, the more understanding, compassionate, and accepting we can become as a society. As Carolyn Boyes-Watson and Kay Pranis say in their book, *Circle Forward*, "When we are using Circle as a regular practice . . . we are practicing basic ways of being that are fundamental to being successful together."

The more we practice circle,
the more we bring
the foundations of circle
to our interactions
outside of circle.

Circle has the power to bring people who have differences together to better understand, appreciate, and trust one another on a deeper, more meaningful level. In circle, multiple truths are shared, and each person's story is validated and treated with dignity. Every participant is equally responsible for ensuring that the rules of circle are honored and contributing to the safe space that is shared.

Trust lines the circle container so that it transforms into a safe vessel to tell the stories that have defined us for so long. The stories that have become narratives that we keep telling ourselves are stories that we can tell and give away in circle. We say that when a story is told, it becomes the story of those who heard it as well. When we tell our stories, we trust others with them. The listeners interpret what they are being told and may add something of themselves to that story. They may add a shared experience, feeling, or observation to that story. Trust allows us to shed stories of blame, shame, and guilt, and begin to appreciate who we are and how we interact with others in a new way.

Listening intently to circle shares, picking up other people's talking pieces, and sending appreciation to all in the circle are examples of micro-affirmations we can exercise during circle. Micro-affirmations are the subtle things we can do to co-create a positive, inclusive, and, therefore, trusting environment. Micro-affirmations create trust through the "stacking and layering of small moments and reciprocal vulnerability over time," as Dr. Brené Brown says. Although they are labeled as "micro," the impact of micro-affirmations is actually macro, with lasting impacts beyond our imagination.

To keep creating trust, especially in circle, we must operate through a growth mindset to move forward, as opposed to a fixed mindset that keeps us stuck. If we feel like we cannot trust others or can never trust certain people, we are operating from a fixed mindset. A growth mindset lifts us above the lower vibrations of bias, fear, and resistance to the higher frequencies of compassion, respect, and innovation.

Scientifically, bonding triggers the release of endorphins in other people, which makes people more generous and trusting towards us. That's why the release of endorphins plays such an important role in bonding friendships as well as communities like circles.

Gina once went to a panel discussion that featured short interview clips of descendants of genocide survivors, as well as clips from people who were from the country that committed the genocide. There was a question-and-answer period immediately following the event, during which many of the audience members shared their personal stories. It was evident that they desired the space to share their experiences and have others listen.

A growth mindset
lifts us above the lower vibrations
of bias, fear, and resistance
to the higher frequencies
of compassion, respect,
and innovation.

After the event, Gina joined a few of the organizers and panelists to share thoughts about how the event went. She suggested that the organizers use circles for future events of this kind to give the audience more time and space to share their personal experiences. None of them had heard of circles before. After she described the process, they invited her to lead a circle right then and there. Spontaneity grows with the trust of circles, even beyond the circle itself.

Because of her agility as a leader, Gina was able to improvise, without openings, prompts, closings, or even a talking piece prepared. The organizers and panelists had been preparing for the event for months and had been discussing the session topic for at least four hours that day already. Yet, they trusted her to help teach them the circle process for another hour of their time. And Gina trusted herself to lead with whatever came up for her.

Gina's ancestors did not come from either of the countries that were involved in the genocide that was discussed that day. However, she could relate to them because her family members faced ethnic discrimination in the face of violence in other countries thousands of miles away from the countries at issue. Gina, like all of us, was holding generational trauma in her body that she was still processing. Their courage, openness, and trust in her to hold space for their stories inspired her to share her story. After the circle, one of the participants came up to her and said, "Thank you for making today even more meaningful."

Take a moment and reflect on these circle prompts
around generational trauma and trust:

Which ancestors would you like
to bring into this circle?
What gifts have your ancestors bestowed upon you?
How have they guided you?
How have they helped you heal?
How does your family history affect how you interact
with others?
How can you trust more?
What would you tell your ancestors if you
could talk to them now?

CHAPTER 7

Appreciating Differences

Here, the center.
There, an open space
of gratitude
for everyone's greatness:
a circle of gifts,
showing up
just as we are,
appreciating differences.

I n the diversity, equity, and inclusion space, which for us includes accessibility, justice, welcoming, and belonging (together, "belonging and inclusion"), we focus on the importance of everyone having a "seat at the table" to foster an environment that gives everyone the tools and opportunities to succeed. It is an environment where everyone has an opportunity to share their perspectives, which are heard, respected, and considered. Appreciation for our contributions doesn't merely invite us, but welcomes us to the circle, which is wider and more welcoming than the table. Circles are a core part of our belonging and inclusion work because they require that we move beyond being invited to the table—to a deeper connection that requires us to examine ourselves and listen to what we may be afraid to discuss at the "table."

As Aida Mariam Davis says in her article "The Problem with Tables": "Visibility and representation at the table do not necessarily translate to power or influence. For too long, oppressed people have asked, demanded, and even pleaded for a seat at the table. The reality, however, is the table was designed by a select few, for a select few. In order for the table to function, it requires that oppressed peoples assimilate, concede some of their humanity, and suffer ongoing indignities." The circle extends itself beyond role, title, privilege, or hierarchy to welcome everyone.

In Native American tradition, there is a saying of gratitude to uplift appreciation as "the words that come before all else." When we summon the synergy of "all our relations" into the circle, we know there is enough space for everyone and everything to be revered. Taking the time to gather together in circle shows gratitude to everyone in the circle before the circle even begins.

The Hopi say that at one point in the past, the truth was a body of knowledge known by all until the circle was broken and the truth divided. In *Calling the Circle,* Baldwin says, "[e]ach clan was given responsibility for a portion of the truth. They were instructed to care for this truth until such time as they could remember their wholeness and reunite the circle. Of course, after a period of time, the clans forgot that they carried only a fraction of truth and began to think they carried the whole truth. They began hoarding it, protecting it, trying to impose it."

Take a moment and ponder on the portion of the truth that you hold. How have you held onto this truth? What portions of the truth do others around you hold, and how have they held onto them?

Circles are an opportunity to unite the diverse perspectives that are all part of the truth. Competition rather than appreciation of differences is fear based on an erroneous interpretation of the universe as being limited in supply. But the truth is that there is enough happiness for everyone. We don't need to dim our lights or stop ourselves from being too bright, too happy, too successful, too visible, too unusual, too vivid, too loud, too different, *too much.*

We should not have to worry about haters who seek to marginalize us when we are being our best. We need to work on releasing any hatred, disagreement, or discord. We need to sing our song, dance our dance, speak our speech, take our stand, and stay our course because that's why we are here. We need to stop limiting ourselves because of other people's opinions. Let us not deprive the universe, others, and, most importantly, ourselves of all we can be.

Everyone has potential that is just waiting to be recognized. Showing appreciation can turn creative potential into positive power. The most appreciative people have a radar for potential that they recognize when others do not, and this potential shines, especially during circle. The appreciation brought out during circle can extend to recognizing strengths outside of circle.

Appreciative people let others know they are valued, bring out the best in others, provide opportunities, inspire, awaken creative energy, provide a sense of direction and integrity, recognize the best, and give the same. They share positive narratives and allow all to tell their stories to build connection, realizing stories hold culture, co-create reality, and build bridges supporting unlimited success.

When we perceive our ability to thrive as limited, we fail to use our talents and abilities to co-create based on our true potential. Have you ever been around someone who believes that they will shine if they make others look bad? When we are aware of our gifts, we have no desire to point out other people's problems—real or imaginary—and instead focus on being our best. However, facing our own problems head-on and recognizing the strengths in ourselves and others foster a growth mindset we can all adopt, starting with a belief in our shared potential.

Here are some ways we can strengthen our relationships with others with appreciation, intention, and grace both within and outside of the circle:

- Praise others, which makes us feel better. What we give always comes back.

o   Be inclusive of others in circle by thinking of ways we can assist with the accomplishment of someone else's goals outside of circle while listening to others' shares. You will be surprised by just how helpful you can be.

o   Share your truth and be proactive about tapping resources to engage and improve.

o   Learn from what other people share and take time to research circle topics.

o   Recognize others' strengths during circle so the space can be one of healing and transformation.

o   Before, during, and after circle, learn the histories of those who have been oppressed and support their cause as much as your own. When one person suffers, we all do.

Generally, a lot of time is spent focusing on the negative—what others do wrong and complaining about it to others—rather than noticing what they do right and celebrating it. A receptive focus is open and invites us to appreciate the contributions of everyone, regardless of who they are and what their background is, thereby welcoming differences.

Appreciation of someone's efforts allows them to feel like they are part of the team and supports the contribution of their thoughts, ideas, and questions without fear of reprisal. When we feel confident in our own abilities, we can be genuinely happy for the success of everyone. In spaces of appreciation, we are encouraged to bring our best selves to our families, friends, workplaces, communities, and every environment we are in. We also feel psychologically safe and as part of a supportive whole — a community that sees us, validates our experience, and actively engages us as part of the team. Additionally, we are not only given an opportunity to participate fully, but our unique contributions are recognized, our gifts are nurtured, and our skills are cultivated. We are given the professional development, encouragement, and training to succeed.

Here are ways to show appreciation during circle:

- o Send greetings to those in circle.
- o Say "thank you" when someone passes you the talking piece.
- o Uplift something that someone else said during circle.
- o Sit next to someone new or someone whom you know is having a difficult time during an in-person circle.
- o Help fellow circle participants if they are having accessibility issues virtually or in person while avoiding crosstalk (*e.g.*, picking up a talking piece if it falls).
- o Share your story, especially if you think it will help someone else.
- o If you are training a group of Circle Keepers, give them a gift for completing the training like a certificate, talking piece, and/or apparel that binds Circle Keepers together.
- o Make eye contact.
- o Pass someone a tissue if it is out of reach for someone who is tearing up during circle.
- o Put your hand on someone's shoulder if they are having a difficult time.

These ways of showing appreciation exemplify the compassion that is both the foundation as well as the catalyst that we need to help create a successful circle. Successful circles in the workplace ultimately contribute to a positive work environment, which not only welcomes everyone but also builds and strengthens a community of belonging. The Circle Keepers' and other circle participants' positive emotions predict and role model the performance of the entire circle. When a Circle Keeper or circle participant shows compassion, care, and support, their behavior is infectious. We are all here to contribute to the well-being of those around us, which is what inclusion is all about.

Regardless of our individual goals and desires, at its core, our purpose is to develop universal compassion for each other. No matter how positive we are, we all have a "negativity bias." We also embody the historical trauma of our ancestors, as well as our own personal experiences that perpetuate stress. Negativity biases can often come up in circle. Therefore, we must recalibrate our emotional alarm system so that we can manage the voices of our own inner critics and create an inclusive mindset that is more grateful than negative. Gratitude helps lift us above the fray of our inner critics to turn them into inner coaches.

Compassion not only reduces stress but also reduces illness. Scientific studies show that patients reduced their hospital stay and subsequent need for medical care through the presence of a more compassionate physician. Compassion is not a weakness but a strength that enhances our capabilities, relationships, and achievements. At its core, compassion is the goal behind all purpose. By expressing compassion, we fulfill our purpose.

Gratefully, just by being present in circle, we are exhibiting compassion by sharing our experiences, holding space for others' stories, passing the talking piece, and deeply reflecting on the prompts.

Our appreciation of ourselves and others has been shown through circles for thousands of years. Our ancestors sat in circle around the fire, deciding important disputes, but also healing disease and celebrating milestones. Circles work because they are in all our DNA. Regardless of your cultural origin, at some point or another, your ancestors sat in circle and made important decisions.

According to the National Human Genome Research Institute, race is a social construct; "all human beings are 99.9% identical in their genetic makeup." Our differences are only superficial experiences that should not divide us but be opportunities for growth, creativity, innovation, and compassion. The powerful realization we have during circle is that regardless of who we are and what we look like, we are even more alike than we are different. When we hear someone else's story, and it resonates with a personal experience that we've had, we realize that we all have stories of love, loss, trauma, healing, joy, and pain.

During a recent presentation on circles, someone shared their experience with a circle around a campfire. There is ample common ground of bonding at a barbeque or similar outing. Cecilia recalls her Girl Scout days of meeting in a clearing of logs formed in circle, roasting marshmallows, making S'Mores, and telling stories, or singing, but most importantly building a community of love. As some would say, "it's not all Kumbaya," but a Kumbaya of peace is far more preferable than toxicity. If we met more frequently in circle, we would build a better capacity for appreciating one another through peace.

The common ground that binds us all is not merely that we all have human desires, needs, and challenges but that we all have an important role to play as we share the same planet. Building safe spaces requires valuing the unique roles that each one of us plays and uplifting the contributions of one another. Circles give us time to see, hear, and appreciate each other. When "I" celebrate "you," we connect with part of the collective whole that includes everyone as one of many expressions representing all that we are. With compassion, we honor others by affirming rather than criticizing, uplifting rather than gossiping, shining our light rather than hiding, risking rather than armoring, thanking rather than dividing, being vulnerable rather than blaming, and supporting rather than shaming.

Gina goes camping in upstate New York with friends for a weekend every autumn. While there, like the ancestors before us, she scours the area to gather sticks for the fire. Her friends Lance and Julie use those sticks to start the fire. Her other friends Mika, Chris, Meg, and David prepare vegetables and meat for dinner and her husband, Barish, cooks food over the fire. They all make important contributions around the fire, which are the same kind of contributions we make in circle around its altar in the center containing our talking pieces.

When we hear someone else's story,
and it resonates with a personal experience
that we've had, we realize
that we all have stories
of love, loss, trauma, healing,
joy, and pain.

By being together, we create an appreciation of the gifts that each contributor brings, which strengthens our sense of connection, community, and cooperation. The immeasurable sense of gratitude for spending even a few days in nature around the fire with trusted friends is like the appreciation of others felt in circle. Both experiences allow participants to stay present in each moment and notice all the gifts and wisdom that everyone brings. No matter what we were dealing with outside of the circle or outside of the campsite, in circle, we are present for one another, which creates continued connection.

In fact, it is said that once in a circle, you remain even if you leave. We have led circle training where participants must miss a session for one reason or another, but when they resume training, the circles are able to convene in appreciation and support for them. Even if they cannot return, their presence remains a part of the synergy of the circle. In effect, circles can be such an important place of appreciative connection that they cannot be broken.

In the belonging and inclusion space, being included at the proverbial table is a constant reference, even though it is not universally recognized as a symbol of equity. In "The Problem with Tables," Davis recalls an African friend's home where there were no tables. She says there "were some pillows and extra lighting, but notably, there was no furniture, not even a table to work at" because, as a disabled person, 'standard' tables would not fit the space or the height she needed." She says, "The very need of a table must be questioned."

Davis says, "The table... represents the status quo, it does not speak to things as they should be or new ways of being and doing." After doing numerous circles remotely, largely out of necessity during the pandemic, we discovered that the real gift of circle can be sustained beyond the physical structure of an actual circle through the cadence of storytelling alone. Storytelling is such a powerful gift of appreciation that its repetitive cadence and order replicates the formation of a circle.

Appreciation circles can also be used. The person holding the piece is silent, and the rest of the circle offers appreciation to the holder of the talking piece. These can be used as openings, closings, or as part of the heart of the circle. As Baldwin shares, "Appreciation helps us define our place on the team, or in the overall vision of an organization or community."

Take a moment and reflect on these circle prompts
on appreciation:

Who or what do you appreciate and why?

What spaces are you grateful for?

How do you take time to
appreciate someone's strengths?

How are you cultivating the skills of those
who don't look like you?

What is one way you can show
appreciation to others daily?

CHAPTER 8

Leaning In

*Circles allow us
to free fall
into a reservoir of courage
never realized before,
finding strength,
leaning in.*

T he thing that makes most people afraid of circles is what gives them courage after they've tried them. In circle, we learn to adapt to being comfortable with not knowing. We are forced to trust ourselves in the most vulnerable of situations because we are sharing some of our secrets in a space that promises to strengthen us. Yet, we have no concept of how this shift will take place, and we are forced to share our truth with complete strangers. Many of us are afraid that we don't know the answers to our challenges, but the answers are in our hearts.

Many indigenous cultures are not overly dependent on what some call "book sense," realizing that the intellect cultivates but one source of wisdom. Use of only the mind in experiencing life is limited. It's not the intellect that allows us to walk into a room and immediately access its energy without anyone saying a word; it's our ability to feel the vibrations of what has taken place. We can be compassionate without saying a single word through the wisdom of the heart. We can even have a deep sense of knowing through our guts, guidance that is triggered by things we have not yet experienced. Circles require us to lean in with a similar dependency on the unseen. We become more in tune with our ability to lean in without knowing, trusting that whatever we need to say will be revealed—not because it is a right answer (there are no right answers in circle) but because it is the truth that needs to be shared at the moment.

Native Americans call on "all relations" in circle, acknowledging that there is a wisdom in circle that is deeper than who we are in the flesh. All relations include the ancestors on whose shoulders we stand. They are not only humans but also plants and animals. Everything and everyone is "related" to us. The illusion of being separate makes us feel disconnected from the power of being one with "all our relations" and the reciprocity of our ability to connect in body, mind, and soul. In circle, we lean into the connection that we have with everyone and everything and begin the powerful process of weaving the rich tapestry of common ground that we share.

When we grow more accustomed to leaning in, leaning in and letting go without trying to control an outcome becomes the norm. By leaning in, we learn to trust whatever comes up for us. This trust in our gut, our instinct, and the guidance of the unseen is what cultivates new ideas, innovation, change, and genius.

◎◎◎◎◎◎◎◎◎◎◎◎◎◎◎◎◎◎◎◎

Native Americans call on
"all relations"
in circle, acknowledging that
there is a wisdom in circle
that is deeper than
who we are in the flesh.

◎◎◎◎◎◎◎◎◎◎◎◎◎◎◎◎◎◎◎◎

The circle is an opening through which we step into a consciousness of connection. Surrendering allows us to understand the greater whole. We are not merely individuals; we are one. When we lean in, we trust and through that trust develop courage.

In the past, we might not have had the courage to tell our story because it might have brought us shame and made us feel less than who we are, but in circle, we are nourished, strengthened, and empowered by the truth that we share together. Our stories unfold through our collective wisdom. We are humbled when we realize we are all similar and all share the common ground of striving to find peace on our journey of learning more about ourselves and each other.

We lean in and discover a mirror. We realize that the circle is not so much made up by those around us but reflects our own truth. By seeing others, we see ourselves more clearly. In the silence of listening, we learn to quiet the thousands of different thoughts that come up for us daily. By leaning in, we reduce those thoughts to a shared pattern of the tapestry of our collective testimonies.

We lean in
and discover a mirror.

Many Black churches, regardless of denomination, begin with testimony from the congregation. "Giving honor to God, who is the head of my life and to his son Jesus the Christ," and right there, with the acknowledgment of a source of spiritual invitation, various stories are shared as the remaining congregation listens with empathy and compassion as congregants stand as a witness, talking about doors opening, opportunities appearing, conflict resolving, health improving, wealth manifesting, and ways being made out of "no way."

Testifying during church includes sharing stories, avid listening, and supportive shouts in the guise of an "Amen," "Hallelujah," or the wave of a hand. With an agile organ player, the challenge and victory of stories might even be underscored by music. We lean into the impossible, and we find that the truth that has brought us to where we are is enough to guide us, and the process of sharing that truth is a reward in and of itself.

Parishioners rise to their feet through the acknowledgment, gratitude, and appreciation of their blessings when they testify. They don't try to control the outcome of their speech or the manner of their expression when they testify. Those testifying "move with the Spirit," trusting the unseen. In fact, Spirit can be so strong in church that leaning in can even be manifested by a holy dance, joyful tears, and/or other forms of releasing the decorum that we try to hold onto.

Circles are similar. The benefit of letting go is that surrender releases our burdens, and we experience more clarity. The restoration is in the release. Once we share the secrets that have been troubling us, we are no longer required to carry them. As Brené Brown shares in her talks on shame: shame cannot survive the sharing of its story.

When we lean in, we receive because we give. We often think about the tangible gifts that we receive when we give but not about how the simultaneous sharing of our story gives itself and receives instantaneously the blessing of its share. We lean in through circle and hold each other with our shared stories, as we learn through the humility of removing the need for pretense and letting go of our masks. There is liberation in being able to speak our truth and accept the collective wisdom of those who have joined to share the stories that have made them who they are.

In circle, we can let go of the ego. Limited to the ego, everything we give is clouded by the artificiality of judgment, self-centeredness, and selfishness. We focus on competition rather than community. In *Caste*, Wilkerson warns us of the danger of not leaning in. She says we do not "look" at our peril. "Whatever is lurking will fester whether [we] choose to look at it or not. Ignorance is no protection from the consequences of inaction." We have to lean in to "gather the courage to face what [we] would rather not [know]."

The circle brings balance, as shown by the Native American circle of the four directions, elements, and seasons. In these higher frequencies of life and greater purpose of being, we are more aligned with the deep spiritual roots of who we are, where we came from, and how the grandparents we may not have known continue to guide us through whatever we experience, including racism, slavery, reservations, camps, and other horrendous forms of genocide. We stand on their vision, hope, love, and strength. When we open ourselves to an awareness of our shared greatness, we tap the power of our ancestors to heal what still needs healing, fix what needs fixing, and accept the unlimited power of the universe as one shared by all.

When we lean in together, regardless of the various paths that we walk, we honor our capacity to be visionary, to leave norms, conventions, and rigidity to create a world that honors everyone. When we lean in, we access the strength of all our relations throughout the world, all cultures, languages, expressions, and traditions, and all that they teach us. When we do not lean into all experiences, we miss the opportunity to experience all aspects of who we are, and we do not give to the parts of us most in need. Leaning in calls us to honor the entirety of who we are and our connection to the entire planet and invites us to care for our whole self by receiving from and giving to all our relations.

We often think about the tangible gifts
that we receive when we give
but not about how the simultaneous sharing
of our story gives itself
and receives instantaneously
the blessing of its share.

As set forth in *The Power of Inclusion*, we do not have the strength to do what needs to be done alone. When we fail to come together and learn from each other in a circle of truth, we live in the toxicity of lower vibrations. Circles give to us the power of higher vibrations because when we welcome, uplift, and honor everyone as equals, we accomplish an important step in welcoming, uplifting, and supporting ourselves.

Our relations have shared teachings throughout time that the balance we need in our lives begins with Spirit. Do you understand the power that you are? By respecting the truth that you are a spiritual being, having an experience in a physical world will not answer all your questions immediately, but it is a starting place. Spirit as our counselor, teacher, and guide shows us the path to heart and meaning. Spirit, or whatever you call higher consciousness—Divine Mind, Absolute Good, God, Jehovah, Allah, I AM, Krishna, Ra, Buddha—provides a fulcrum for achieving balance that is not lost but is found in circle.

All civil rights movement leaders were anointed with the unlimited power of Spirit to accomplish their work. There is no question that Rev. Dr. Martin Luther King, Jr. was a man of Spirit. Harriet Tubman was a woman of Spirit. Nelson Mandela was a man of Spirit. Gandhi was a man of Spirit. Malcolm X was a man of Spirit. The work of inclusion, racial equity, and justice, welcoming and uniting everyone, is not merely a physical battle; it is spiritual work. Spirit is essential to our balance and ability to cross the finish line of success.

When we lean into circle, we recognize that the power of Spirit does not divide us according to how we choose to experience our religious culture or creed but is the essential first step that we must make, guided by the truth that awakens us. Dr. King was Christian; Gandhi was Hindu; Malcolm X was Muslim; Jesus was Jewish, but all shared the inexhaustible Spirit that gave them the enlightenment, fortitude, and miracles that they needed.

It is not a coincidence that many of our circles begin with a devotional, prayer, or meditation, centering on the greatness of Spirit expressing as us. When we lean into the circle with Spirit, we experience healing because we are already whole. We are already one, not only one person who is one with all attributes of mind, body, and soul, but we are also one people united beyond the caste-based world that we inhabit. When we lean into circle, we know that we are more together than apart and show up as our powerful best selves, filled with the light, presence, and truth of the kindred unity of connection.

In circle, we are blessed by what we do not know and inevitably discover about ourselves. When we sat in circle for five days, healing took place that could not be measured, but the impact of something being lifted and removed was evident. We can circle for an hour or two and have a similar experience simply because we step outside of our own limited consciousness and dare to experience the greatness of the unknown, which in turn reveals all that we are here to do.

The following prompts can guide us in circle to be
open to new ways of creating a greater
capacity to lean into our own truth.

What are some of your triggers
and how do you regulate them?

If you had the power to change the world,
what would you do?

How can you support those who are treated
less than you?

III.

A CIRCLE OF
TRANSFORMATION

Circles are answered prayers,
waiting for
whatever comes up,
grateful to be a center
where we
can always return.

CHAPTER 9

Healing Harm

Circles open spaces,
breaking ties
that bind us
to the past,
letting go of hurt,
releasing others,
healing harm.

One of the most important gifts of circle is an opportunity to heal. Healing harm requires that we be provided a safe space to be vulnerable and share our truth, to also provide others with the opportunity to do so and perhaps find common ground, increase our wisdom, and see beyond our differences to the good of all humanity. Everyone is harmed at some point, and everyone experiences harming others. All our experiences regarding harm are processed to not only be healed and to protect against future attacks but also to limit our own propensity to harm others.

In *Caste*, Wilkerson shares the story of a Black nine-year-old boy who was accused of sexually assaulting a 53-year-old White woman in a deli in Flatbush, Brooklyn. Her prejudice of vehemence against Black people was so vile and distorted that she accused this small male child of African descent of violating her sexually. Fortunately, there were cameras in the store that were viewed afterwards and the video tape recording of what she claimed was an attack revealed that the small child was carrying a bag that accidentally brushed against the woman. She later apologized, but he refused to forgive her, saying she had a problem and needed help.

Healing does not require forgiveness nor the need to forget injustices suffered. Similarly, in healing circles, forgiveness is not required. Instead, we co-create a safe space to open the wounds of harm: to explore how we feel, to be with our pain, to surrender to the truth of what took place, and if we are fortunate—to restore, repair, and renew our commitment as healing agents for the world. The latter, however, is a personal choice. As the Lady in Red says in Ntozake Shange's play *For Colored Girls Who Have Committed Suicide/When the Rainbow is Enuf*, "One thing I don't need is any more apologies. I got sorry greetin' me at my front door, you can keep yours. I don't know what to do wit' 'em."

Circles are for both harmer and harmed and the shame that both endure. Shame researcher and author Dr. Brené Brown defines shame as "the intensely painful feeling or experience of believing that we are flawed and therefore unworthy of love and belonging," which also invokes fear. Neuroscience research concludes that the pain and feelings of rejection that shame inflicts are as real as physical pain.

Derek R. Brookes, author of *Beyond Harm: Toward Justice, Healing and Peace,* shares that shame threatens the social aspect of ourselves in terms of how we perceive ourselves and how we think others perceive us. Anytime we forgive or ask for forgiveness, shame is felt either by us and/or the person we harmed.

We have all experienced shame in our lives and still do. Shame affects all human beings and has a strong impact on our lives, whether we like to admit its existence and influence or not. If we do not acknowledge its existence, shame can have an extremely detrimental effect on our well-being, as it is highly correlated to addiction, depression, violence, aggression, suicide, and eating disorders. As much as we try not to allow it to dwell or flourish, shame can be triggered by specific memories or by subtle messages that can stay with us for a lifetime.

When we are in circle, a prompt or story may remind us of a memory or experience that brings up shame. The first steps to releasing shame are to be aware of feelings that arouse it and understand why that memory brings up the feeling of shame. Recognizing that everyone has shame and that we are not alone in it helps us to heal and talk about it with others.

Recognizing that everyone has shame
and that we are not alone in it
helps us to heal
and talk about it with others.

In circle, we can combat shame by sharing our stories, expressing self-compassion, and trusting the circle process. All these steps move us toward healing. The circle process, which doesn't allow for crosstalk, empowers each participant to share their story to the extent that they feel comfortable doing so without interruptions or judgment from other participants. The courage it takes for someone to be vulnerable enough to share their story around shame can inspire others in the circle to do the same.

Participating in circle is one of the bravest things we can do because there is no hiding behind superficialities in circle: everyone is required to bring their authentic selves to circle and face their truths. Participants can also share positive affirmations, known as "speaking truth to power," to transform the inner critic associated with shame to an inner coach. When more circle participants express similar feelings, experiences, or stories, they feel more validated and less alone, thus decreasing feelings associated with shame and increasing trust.

Circles on more challenging topics, like the caste system and ingrained prejudice, require a strong foundation amongst the participants for their circle to be a healing space. It can be challenging to share experiences around these topics with people you do not know well. Therefore, it is important to build community and trust amongst circle participants first before introducing prompts on triggering topics. Otherwise, participants will not feel as open, comfortable, or safe enough to share.

When we conduct our seven-week Circle Keepers Training, the first two weeks include circles focused on getting to know one another better and learning about emotional intelligence. Shame is usually the third week's topic, and forgiveness is discussed during the fourth week.

As Bishop Desmond Tutu sets forth in *The Book of Forgiving*, "Forgiveness is not a weakness; it is a strength. It requires bravery and strength to release people and situations who have harmed us." It may be easier to hold a grudge than to forgive someone. Whether we are forgiven or not, we will always live with the consequences of our actions. Processing forgiveness is not quick; it does not require us to forget, deny, or pretend that something did not happen. Forgiveness does not deny history nor refrain from seeking justice. Rather, forgiveness puts us on a path toward healing ourselves, our local communities, and the global community at large.

Similarly, healing is not about traumatized people taking a higher road; it is about those who hold power owning their mistakes and facing their inadequacies. Healing circles are not about absolving a perpetrator for misdeeds or harmed people demonstrating an almost supernatural nobility to endure mistreatment and suffer abuse but about embracing our pain and having a space to unpack the truth.

Healing is about putting ourselves first. We have the power to decide what makes us whole. Perhaps it is a boundary rather than continued interaction, or accountability and release. Circles are available to address all kinds of harm, including those we experience within our families, at our workplaces, in our communities, and the greater world at large. Healing requires everyone to confront their own demons and how a failure to be compassionate, have patience, or listen with grace may have harmed themselves as well as others.

Sometimes people will not accept us for who we are; however, that is not necessarily a sign we need to change. We cannot change other people; they do that for themselves. What we can change is how we allow others to impact our lives.

Circles help us with the process of healing. When we hear other participants' stories about healing, they help us learn how we can heal. Healing is about us taking care of ourselves, having a space where we can speak out against indignities and/or be accountable for how we may have disrespected or disregarded by others. When we sit in circle, open to the depth of truth, we connect with a new synergy of awareness, given the courage it takes to speak about how we have harmed or been harmed with candor. Healing opens spaces that were closed with a greater capacity to love, heal, and *be* different.

Forgiveness does not deny history
nor refrain from seeking justice.

Circles can help us if we would like to heal through the process of forgiveness. When we hear other participants' stories about forgiveness, they remind us of times we forgave others and the impact the act of forgiving has on our lives. Circles are also an invaluable tool for reminding us of the people and situations for whom we need to process forgiveness. When we allow ourselves to sit in circle, open to the depth of truth, we connect with a new synergy of awareness, reminded of those who have forgiven us and how forgiveness not only impacts our lives but also those around us. When we witness other circle participants' courage to speak about their experiences with forgiveness, we are inspired to forgive. Forgiveness can open spaces that were closed with a greater capacity to love, heal, and see life differently.

In his book *Happiness: A Guide to Developing Life's Most Important Skill*, Ricard Matthieu, one of the world's most learned experts on happiness, says that "while it may be difficult to change the world, it is always possible to change the way we look at it." Hatred for others harms us even more than them and adversely impacts our happiness because we are "biologically, cognitively, physically, and spiritually wired to love, to be loved, and to belong," as Dr. Brené Brown says. Whatever the challenge, we need to speak our pain, stand in our power to choose, and be passionate about our greatness.

Healing releases the energy that is blocked by the past—through speaking, hearing, processing, grieving, acknowledging, and changing for the better. When we assault another's humanity, we assault our own humanity. Bishop Tutu said, "[e]very person wants to be acknowledged and affirmed for who and what they are, a human being of infinite worth, someone with a place in the world. We can't violate another's dignity without violating our own. Violence, whether in words or deeds, only begets more violence. Violence can never engender peace." Restorative practices heal both harmer and harmed, which allows us to create a space for acknowledging restoration, release, and renewal.

Research shows that ruminating about grudges is just as stressful as the actual experience. When we continue holding a grudge against someone, that negativity can be contagious and all-consuming. If you allow it, resentment can take up residence in your heart and be so ingrained in your psyche that it can affect your relationships with others, including your family members. It can manifest into intergenerational trauma so pervasive that even if family members did not personally experience that event, they also feel its negative effects for generations to come.

Forgiveness does not involve excusing another person's actions or forgetting what happened. To forgive is not the same as to reconcile. Reconciliation is a negotiation strategy in which two or more people come together again in mutual trust. You may choose not to reconcile with the person you are forgiving. Forgiveness is letting go of your emotional ties to the past so that you can move forward, unencumbered, into the future. Telling our stories is part of the way that we process forgiveness and decide whether to reconcile. What we choose to do and how we proceed is a process that unfolds at the heart of the stories we tell and the insight we gain from them.

During circles on forgiveness, some participants share that they have chosen not to forgive someone. It's important to remember that some people are easier to forgive than others, which varies from person to person and from time to time, depending on the situation. We say that "the circle takes care of itself" so if conflict or discord does come up, following the rules of circle is critical to fix what's been broken. When we are in a circle and are reminded of harm being done that is very severe, it may take multiple rounds or circles to get to a point of forgiveness. We may also never reach a point of forgiveness, and that is okay. Circles help us address the roots of the issues so we can honor our path towards creative solutions, inside or outside of circle.

If we are in circle with someone who we need to forgive or ask forgiveness from, we can dig deeper beyond the iceberg of a problem that has come between our relationship. Circles help reveal the underlying issues that may have exacerbated the problem in the first place. In our daily interactions with people, we only see "the tip of the iceberg," which is only a small part of an issue or of someone's identity, such as behaviors, language, customs, etc. When we pass the talking piece in circle, we see each other for what is below the surface of the iceberg: the beliefs, values, assumptions, desires, and attitudes that are driving our behavior. Afterward, when we see each other outside of the circle, we understand one another on a deeper level as human beings who each have our own lenses through which we see the world and move through, expanding our capacities to put down our walls and forgive more.

Gina shares a story about forgiveness:

> I was once in circle with another participant whose family member was sick. They had been taking care of their loved ones for several months, taking them to doctor's appointments. While she was sharing, I remember feeling so much admiration for this participant's dedication and care to be there for her family members.
>
> Her story brought up an experience for me when I could not be physically present for a loved one when they were sick. It is something I have felt shameful of for many years. I felt guilty that I could not be as physically present, even though I was emotionally present, for them. Years later, I learned that there are many ways to be there for the ones that you love, not just physically. This realization helped me forgive myself.
>
> I started to write a letter to my past self, seeking forgiveness. I also apologized to my loved

one and realized that I was harboring much more guilt toward myself compared to how much disappointment I thought my loved one was holding. They quickly forgave me. This is just one example of how listening to others' stories helps us heal, forgive, and strengthen our relationships.

Cecilia's ministry includes a theology of forgiveness, which establishes that this healing mechanism supports self-empowerment. Members exchange text messages regarding daily reminders about release as a source of liberation. In an informal circle, each weekly lesson includes a gathering where members share stories and provide testimony about healing through release for the pain caused by family, friends, colleagues, culture, and/or the world at large. Annually, there are opportunities to forgive, release, and let go—either through letters, affirmations, or burning bowls of baggage that have been carried far too long.

Circles will inevitably reflect a variety of faiths. Most faiths support a theology of forgiveness, whether based on the teachings of Jesus Christ or not. Thích Nhất Hanh called lack of forgiveness "habit energy." In *Together We Are One: Honoring Our Diversity, Celebrating Our Connection*, he said: "Suppose. . . you realize that the thought you produced yesterday was not right thinking. You are now determined to produce the kind of thought that is full of compassion, understanding, and forgiveness. This thought also bears your signature. As soon as you have produced this thought, it will pursue the angry thought from yesterday and transform it. The Buddha teaches that because nothing is lost, you can repair the past. The thought you produced yesterday is your continuation. You do not want your continuation to be angry, you want it to be beautiful."

Forgiveness is similarly discussed in other faiths. In the Bhagavad Gita, Lord Krishna declares forgiveness to be a requirement for liberation and is contrasted with the anger and resentment that keep us in bondage. The Torah says that when asked for forgiveness, one should forgive. Forgiveness is mentioned many times in the Qur'an. The Native American Great Spirit says there needs to be great forgiveness. Most, if not all, faiths recognize that unconditional love, which includes forgiveness, is critical to healing ourselves, which does not require us to reconcile with other people, but it does require us to make peace with ourselves.

In *The Little Book of Racial Healing*, Thomas Norman DeWolf says that "[s]itting in circle with other people committed to racial healing and exploring touchstones and values is a form of taking action. Becoming knowledgeable about trauma and its impact and learning to be resilient in the face of trauma is a form of taking action." When we give ourselves time to be fully present in circle, radical healings take place. But most people don't give themselves the requisite time that they need to heal. It's easy to complain about initiatives in diversity, equity, inclusion, and belonging not being effective. Yet, to heal, we have to be willing to take the time that it takes to heal and do the work that's necessary to see results. It's just like reaching fitness goals. You can't do one exercise class and expect to change your physique. Circles are part of the healing work that we all need to do.

In *Radical Forgiveness: A Revolutionary Five-Stage Process to Heal Relationships, Let Go of Anger and Blame, and Find Peace in Any Situation*, Colin Tipping shares that in the Navajo circle, the aggrieved could air their grievance three times, while everyone listened with empathy and compassion. On the fourth occasion, however, when the aggrieved came into the circle, everyone turned their backs, saying "Enough! We have heard you express your concern three times. We have received it. Now let it go. We will not hear it again," which served as a powerful ritual of support for letting go of past pain. This release is not for others, it's for ourselves.

Many have successfully used circles based on the Navajo tradition with the confidence that circles have healing power. We recognize that healing takes place in many ways, through letter-writing, breathwork, burning bowls, study, faith, walking, and acknowledging release. Regardless of how it's done, circles can be an amazing contribution to the process of healing, and just as importantly, healing and all its various components, like forgiveness, reconciliation, and/or release are an invaluable catalyst for change.

Who or what do you need to heal?

How has forgiveness, release or reconciliation
impacted your experiences and ability to show
up as your best?

Who do you wish could forgive you?

How can you grow so that you create fewer
situations that require forgiveness?

Discovering Empathy

Circles like wind
blow breezes,
summon energy,
hold truth,
carry stories,
binding us,
discovering empathy.

The power of circles is their ability to teach us empathy. Empathy is the ability to identify and understand another person's emotions and feel what they are experiencing from their frame of reference. Every moment in circle is an opportunity to express empathy for ourselves and others. Empathy allows us to see ourselves clearly, to understand others accurately, and to communicate those perceptions with compassion. Empathy requires us to speak from the heart of our own experience.

Arthur P. Ciaramicoli, author of *The Power of Empathy*, says that "heartless truth-telling is not the way of empathy." In circle, we do not use "heartless truth-telling." Empathy "signifies a commitment to set aside our theories and biases so that we can enter every new situation with an open mind—the beginner's mind that Zen practitioners talk about," says Ciaramicoli.

Both empathy and sympathy connect us to the experiences of others with emotion, but they are not to be confused with one another. Sympathy is feeling sorrow or pity for the hardships that someone else is experiencing, while empathy goes one step further by imagining yourself in the other person's situation. In *Caste*, Wilkerson talks about "radical empathy," which is putting in the work to educate oneself and to listen with a humble heart to understand another's experience from their perspective, not as we imagine we would feel." Wilkerson calls "radical empathy," the "kindred connection from a place of deep knowing that joins your Spirit to the power of another as they feel."

In their book *Compassionate Leadership: How to Do Hard Things in a Human Way*, Rasmus Hougaard and Jacqueline Carter teach us that empathy is important because it "enables us to connect with other human beings." But empathy and compassion are different: "compassion is empathy plus action."

Hougaard and Carter teach that "[e]mpathy is the ability to feel with another being." They say research establishes that "empathy increases life satisfaction, emotional intelligence, and self-esteem. People with high empathy have larger and more ful-filling social networks, are more social themselves, volunteer more readily, donate more to charity, and are more likely to help others in need." Empathy is an important aspect of emotional in-telligence, but self-awareness, self-regulation, and pro-social behavior are the other important aspects of emotional intelli-gence that support change.

In the 2020 edition of *Circle Forward: Building a Restorative School Community*, Kay Pranis and Carolyn Boyes-Watson share that circle preparation and prompts help "provide questions [that] are designed to build community, deepen relationships, and develop empathy." When others are listening with curiosity and understanding without responding, this becomes a true practice of expressing empathy. Thus, we can create the right prompts in order to facilitate more empathy, which is what we do when we use smaller circles structured to provide coaching.

Circles help increase empathy by helping us listen more than we speak, allowing us to share our stories, helping us be more vulnerable, moving us beyond assumptions to truth, and in-creasing the connectivity that we need to bond and trust in relationships.

Neuroscientists have supporting evidence for empathy, find-ing that when we witness what others are experiencing, we activate our own emotions, sensations, and actions as if we are experiencing the same thing. Psychiatrist Bessel Van Der Kolk, M.D. and author of *The Body Keeps the Score*, shares that, "feeling listened to and understood changes our physiology; being able to articulate a complex feeling, and having our feelings recognized, lights up our limbic brain and creates an 'aha moment.' In contrast, being met by silence and incomprehension kills the spirit." Our bodies help us to connect empathetically with others.

⊚⊚⊚⊚⊚⊚⊚⊚⊚⊚⊚⊚⊚⊚⊚⊚⊚⊚

Sympathy is feeling sorrow or pity for the hardships that someone else is experiencing, while empathy goes one step further by imagining yourself in the other person's situation.

⊚⊚⊚⊚⊚⊚⊚⊚⊚⊚⊚⊚⊚⊚⊚⊚⊚⊚

Empathy requires radical listening, which is a practice of listening intently to others while quieting the mind and leaving all our biases at the door. Rita Charon, founder and executive director of the Narrative Medicine Program at Columbia University, says that radical listening is "the kind of listening that allows listeners to accept what tellers tell as having credibility—even if the tale is alien, foreign, or rubs again at the listeners' own positions." When we listen more with the intent of being curious as opposed to judgment, we start to see others as individuals instead of tying them to a negative stereotype, assumption, or preconceived notion we had about them.

Empathy also requires patience. In circle, we are always observing and listening, constantly to ourselves and to each other. We are taking more time observing than reacting, listening than speaking, and asking questions than answering them. Circles also help us to understand and realize our purpose and align our collective visions, which takes time. In speaking our truths, we grow to feel even more confident in our own voices and liberated by what we share.

Gina shares an experience with empathy through an activity like a circle:

> When I was halfway through my Peace Corps service, I helped organize a fishbowl activity session that all the volunteers in China were invited to participate in. We had multiple fishbowls, which were small groups of volunteers who sat in a circle and shared their experiences as someone who identified with a particular race/ethnicity.
>
> For example, the first fishbowl round focused on volunteers who identified as Black or African American; the second round was made up of those who identified as Asian; the third round focused on those who identified as White, and so on. A facilitator introduced prompts for the fishbowl volunteers to reflect on and share responses to, and they passed the microphone, which served as the talking piece, around the circle. The other people in the room sat around the fishbowl, listening to what was shared, and could not respond. After all the fishbowl rounds, we divided up into small

groups that were each made up of both fish-
bowl participants and observers to discuss tips
on how to be better allies for one another.

⊚⊚⊚⊚⊚⊚⊚⊚⊚⊚⊚⊚⊚⊚⊚⊚⊚

In speaking our truths, we grow to feel even more confident in our own voices and liberated by what we share.

⊚⊚⊚⊚⊚⊚⊚⊚⊚⊚⊚⊚⊚⊚⊚⊚⊚

This activity allowed us to truly understand
the experiences of those of different races/eth-
nicities and allowed us to be more empathetic
and supportive of one another the following
year. I had my own challenges with being an
Asian American volunteer in China (*e.g.*, being
marginalized because I did not look like the
"typical American"), and upon sharing my experience, other members of my cohort actively
reached out to support me. It was a learning
experience for me as well to learn about others'
challenges and how to support them. The fish-
bowl activity provided this space where the
volunteers felt empowered, comfortable, and

heard, and the observers were accepting, em-pathetic, and eager to listen.

Leading this affinity group, and especially this activity, felt incredibly rewarding. I wanted to continue this type of work upon re-turning to the United States, so I created my own graduate degree program in DEI. A prac-tice like circle helped lead me to my purpose, and it has the power to lead you through yours as well.

Some of the most challenging experiences to share that re-quire empathy are those deeply triggering experiences around race, politics, and religion. But when a safe space is created to share, we realize that the human connectivity of heart and com-passion provides the connective tissue we need to grow communities of understanding.

When Cecilia met with hundreds of Captains or "Company Commanders" at FDNY in small groups of 20-25 members of the Department over several months, empathy shaped a container for what they needed to listen, learn, and understand the co-cre-ation of a positive and holistic work environment. As the Chief Diversity and Inclusion Officer, Cecilia honored the experiences that they all shared by first tapping their ability to empathize with her journey.

⊚⊚⊚⊚⊚⊚⊚⊚⊚⊚⊚⊚⊚⊚⊚⊚⊚⊚

When a safe space is created to share,
we realize that the human connectivity
of heart and compassion provides
the connective tissue we need to grow
communities of understanding.

⊚⊚⊚⊚⊚⊚⊚⊚⊚⊚⊚⊚⊚⊚⊚⊚⊚⊚

"I sat in the center of the room," Cecilia says, "and asked the Company Commanders to ask me whatever they wanted to know about me. When I showed vulnerability, they empathized with the recent loss of my father, my presence at the World Trade Center in 1993 when it was bombed, and my pride at seeing them put their lives on the line climbing 70-80 flights of stairs with heavy gear as we went down." She says, "I walked around the room and asked each one of them why they were number one when it came to responding to emergencies and how they provided the leadership to build successful teams. After they shared things like authentic trust, supportive relationships, positive practices like mindfulness, excellent training and preparation, community engagement, and the dedicated success of accountability, I said, 'Now you've just told me what diversity and inclusion are about.'"

Shared stories were already customary around the kitchen table, which is what made Cecilia realize the importance of circles in a first responder culture. "One of the most important things that one of the Hispanic lieutenants had me do as soon as I got in the role of Chief Diversity and Inclusion Officer was to go through a series of the physical tests that the firefighters had to perform to be hired. In that way, not only would they be able to see me, but I could most definitely see and empathize with them. When I shared the story of taking the Functional Skills Test, they were more empathetic with me as well."

A significant aspect of what was shared in circle around the firehouse table while meals were prepared, stories were shared, food was blessed, bread was broken, and dishes were put in the dishwasher were the values that contributed to the work and the common ground that everyone shared regardless of race or background: Honor, Bravery, Safety, Service, Preparedness, and Dedication. After sitting in circle around the kitchen table one day, a White senior firefighter, who was about to retire after over 30 years, said that throughout his entire tenure, no one had come to the firehouse to listen to them. Belonging and inclusion, which is a broad way of describing the need to empathize as well as uplift everyone—especially those who are marginalized—begins with our ability to listen to all perspectives.

Some of the most powerful circles witnessed were with firefighters and fire officers, who were being trained as Circle Keepers, showing vulnerability and empathy as a sign of strength rather than weakness. We learned together that when we are in circle, whether it be at roll call, around the kitchen table, or on virtual circle calls with the top brass, we practice empathy by respecting whatever comes up for others.

Sometimes in circle, people are inspired to provide a view that is not required by the prompt, so they share by using a different version of the question based on what comes up for them, which is acceptable if the general theme in the circle is respected. We empathize with wherever each person is on their journey. Even when someone passes or just holds the talking piece in silence, we respect what comes up for them and try to imagine how they may be experiencing the circle at that moment.

Empathy opens the door to impact. One of the ways to take empathy one step further is to use it as a catalyst for mentoring. Over the last 35 years, Cecilia mentored countless students and young professionals. To her surprise, at an event at New York Law School, her mentee Zaniah Maynor asked people who had received the benefit of her mentoring to stand. The number of people who stood and the variety of their accomplishments was amazing. The impact of your contributions when your focus is on giving rather than receiving is greater. Circles allow us to give the gift of empathy by allowing us to give more to others simultaneously.

Gina's Peace Corps Country Director who was a teacher for decades prior to becoming Director, said, "I may never know the impact that I have had on some of my students' lives who I taught many years ago, and that is okay." There is no question that one of the most important contributions he made to his students was being empathetic by seeing, hearing, and valuing their journeys. In circles, empathy is built into the structure of shares but can be followed by actual support and giving even more time. Mentoring circles can be used to build a foundation for getting to know multiple people, which can intentionally be used to share insight and build a community of support.

Someone else's story may deepen
your awareness of a truth
you never understood
or give you the courage
to make a transformational shift
you didn't realize needed to be made.

Like the experiences we have with mentors and teachers who touch our lives, circles impact us during our shares or long after they have taken place. You may never know the impact of what you said during circle on someone's life unless they tell you. Someone else's story may deepen your awareness of a truth you never understood or give you the courage to make a transformational shift you didn't realize needed to be made. Because of another's share, we may be inspired to learn more about a subject, read a new book, forgive someone who wronged us, apply a new leadership skill, incorporate a meditation technique, or listen to our loved ones with more compassion. We may not be able to measure the impact of our story, but it can still change someone's life forever, especially when we speak our truth with empathy.

Some of the most powerful circles that enhance empathy are those that allow us to share about our childhood. Memories about traditions that others grew up with or about people who inspired us, like our ancestors, help develop deep connections in our minds with our own memories, families, and influences. The talking pieces that we use also give context to our stories. Sometimes we may even recall someone's talking piece without remembering all aspects of what was shared.

Talking pieces invite other people's energies and our memories of them into the circle. The talking pieces carry spirit, wisdom, strength, beauty, and pain for others in circle to learn from. We enjoy bringing new talking pieces to circles so that people can learn more about us and we can develop a different and/or more emotional connection with the talking pieces. We can also bring in talking pieces that remind us of something that we are still processing or need healing from so that we can change the narrative around what the talking pieces or the memories they are tied to mean to us.

Shawn Stevens (Red Eagle) taught us about the universal empathy that all of us beings have for one another at Kripalu Center for Yoga & Health ("Kripalu"). Stevens is an enrolled member of the Stockbridge Munsee band of Mohicans and who, among many roles, is a musician, historian, and sharer of knowledge. He shared Native history and traditions with us, emphasizing the respect that we should have for all living things. If we look at our evolution as a people on this planet, we have become more and more disconnected from our ancestors, cultural heritages, and traditions. At the same time, new generations want to learn from their elders. How we treat the earth is also how we treat ourselves and the next generations who will inherit it: acknowledging this responsibility underscores our commitment to leave the world "no less but greater than we found it," which is the Ephebic Oath that Gina often recited in high school. Participating in circles will help us leave the world greater than we found it because sharing our stories, being in community with one another, and creating space for listening are gifts we are always giving. In a sense, we take a silent oath when we show up for circle: to be honest, to be objective, and to be empathetic. By so doing, we have already begun the process of improving the world.

How do you express empathy outside of circle?

Whom can you express more
empathy to?

How do you leave the
world no less but greater
than you found it?

Designing Circles

Finding themes,
spotting issues,
resolving conflicts,
healing hurts,
sharing truths,
telling stories,
designing circles.

I t doesn't matter what our needs are, we can find a way to address them in circle. Circles are as dynamic as we are. Circles encompass whatever we put inside of them. Circles are just as beneficial to one person as they are to another. Circles are containers for processing whatever comes up without bias, fault, or constraint. Circles are generous; they will meet us where we are and bend to whatever weight we need to contain the hurt, the grief, the pain, the joy, the lessons, the life, the commitment, the conflict, or whatever else we need to put in its center. So, the good news is that we can design whatever circle we want, and it will be effective as long as we are sincere with our intention and follow the circle rules. If we don't follow the rules, we're not in circle.

We have participated in circles of hundreds of people or as few as three. We participated in circles that lasted all day or even all week. We have participated in circles that lasted 12 or even 14 weeks. We have participated in circles with many keepers as part of a city-wide event. We have participated in circles for city agencies, the mayor's office, and circles of hundreds of women convening on a floor to address the importance of women of color. No matter what the need, circles are strong enough to hold space, transforming from a mere configuration into a space of empowerment where we can lay down our burdens and be renewed.

When circles are done in person, the center becomes the altar, which is filled with the relics of our past, the values and purpose we hold, and the unseen potential that bridges them to a future of infinite possibilities. Altars are where we worship but also where we release and develop the capacity to pay homage to one another by sharing lessons from everyone's stories. At the altar, we invoke collective wisdom and share truth beyond what we know individually, not praying for things but for the insight that empowers us to see beyond our current circumstances, to realize our own power, to improve our capacity for emotional intelligence, and to cultivate change.

Outside of circle, we generally do not listen to each other, especially to those who have less power and influence. We do not listen because we have the privilege of not doing so. But if we do not listen, we are deaf to our detriment, failing to discern what needs to be done to be better for each other and to innovate the changes we so desperately need. Circles help level the playing field so that all voices are heard. The perspectives, viewpoints, ideas, and stories shared in circle are the gifts that need to be heard to reshape, re-envision, and recreate a world that encourages everyone to excel.

Gratefully, circles move us beyond one perspective or a single narrative to cultivate change through the connection of all truth. So, we can use circles to raise the voices of those generally not heard, provide missing perspectives of those outside of the dominant "caste," and design new mechanisms for all voices as well as innovate new tools for transformation. Even those who are not circle participants benefit from the shifts in consciousness of those who do.

Part of the magic inherent in this "gift that keeps giving" is its ability to serve almost any purpose. This chapter provides examples of some of the ways that you can design circles to help cultivate change. Before we provide several examples, one of the most important things to remember is the circle rules. With circle rules, you can design a circle that best serves your needs.

The following is a quick review of the circle rules set forth in more detail above:

- Respect the talking piece: everyone has a turn; no crosstalk, even in the chat—if it's virtual.
- Speak from your heart: only your truth, your perspectives, your experiences.
- Listen deeply: be patient; what is important may be revealed through others.
- Trust that you will know what to say: no need to rehearse mentally.
- Don't ramble: be concise and considerate of the time of others (3 minutes).
- Keepers put the speaking order in the chat.
- Keepers lead the opening and closing, emphasize the rules, and give the prompts; when there are 2-3 keepers, you can share tasks.
- Keepers ensure that everyone takes responsibility for making the circle a welcome, safe place for open dialogue.
- Use your spirit, energy, love, or whatever gives you strength to help hold a space that is clear, open, respectful, and free.
- Keepers can emphasize that "we all have important experiences and something to offer."
- Keepers can generate respect by noting, "We all have something to learn from each other."
- When there is extra time, keepers can just ask, "Is there anything else that comes up for you based on what's been shared?"

- Keepers can respond to a powerful share by modeling a pause to give the circle the opportunity to feel the power of what's been shared.
- Keepers should note that sometimes silence is more powerful than words.

Talking circles provide a basic circle structure that can be used to serve any purpose based on truth that needs to be discussed.

1 - Basic Talking Circles

Talking Circles are not formed to attempt to bring a group to consensus or resolve conflict but to allow everyone to speak about a topic from the participants' perspective. We use talking circles for meetings, check-ins, and roll calls. They can also be used at the end of videos, movies, speakers, and other presentations for reflections. They can be used to provide feedback to a leader or facilitator of a group process, input to decision-makers, or dialogue about community or social concerns.

In the workplace, it is important to provide structure and organization to the talking circles so that there are not too many people per circle, whether live or in person. For remote talking circles on Zoom, numerous circles can occur simultaneously in break-out rooms. It is preferable to organize the talking circles upfront, especially when there will be numerous circles. We always organize at least one or more circle keepers for each break-out circle.

Like Talking Circles, Teaching Circles provide a basic circle structure that can be used to serve any educational purpose that needs to be prioritized.

2 - Teaching Circles

Teaching Circles include the use of circles to teach a variety of subjects. In the belonging and inclusion space, we use them to teach emotional intelligence, mindfulness and implicit bias, psychological safety, micro-aggressions, and micro-affirmations, as well as positive and appreciative leadership. The most important thing about teaching circles is to build safe containers as the circles begin, providing an understanding of circle rules. The openings, closings, and prompts are then used to impart the lessons. These circles can be done as one session, a series of circles over time, or a partial or full-day retreat.

One of the benefits of teaching circles is that insight, processing, and reflection on the lesson are done simultaneously.

With each round, feedback and a better understanding of the material covered are shared and reinforced.

Like Teaching Circles, Healing Circles provide a basic circle structure that can be used to serve any situation or condition that needs to be healed. We are not experts on Native American circles that are traditionally performed for illnesses. Please consult our Resources at the end of the book for references that might be helpful. Here is Yomi's Circle for Healing Toxic Work Environments.

3 - Yomi's Circle for Healing Toxic Work Environments

Abayomi Ajaiyeoba, also known as "Yomi," a DEI expert and circle keeper who worked closely with us at FDNY, has also used circles for "navigating workplace toxicity." She says that "when parties enter circle, they often bring with them aspects of their relationships or dynamics that are fragmented or in need of repair. Sometimes, the underlying issues are elusive, making them hard to identify actions or behaviors precisely. We recognize that individuals bring elements into the circle that require attention and healing. Circles thus become platforms for bridging understanding, encouraging open communication, and fostering vulnerability."

Yomi is also an advocate of "a purposeful pause" at the beginning of circle. She says, "as participants breathe in, they can acknowledge their presence in the circle, trusting in the safety and support of the moment." She guides circles by saying that "As you breathe in, acknowledge your presence in the circle. Trust that you are safe and supported. This pause is vital for releasing any negative energy and creating space for constructive dialogue." Yomi ends her meditation with an affirmation, such as "in this circle, we seek understanding, healing, and resolution that will move us forward," which solidifies the circle as a space for healing and growth.

To ground participants in the circle's purpose, Yomi invites them "to reflect on their journey to their current role and their proudest moments. This reflection helps in reconnecting with the meaningful work they do and the organization's strengths, laying a foundation for collaboration." When exploring issues, these healing circles "delve into concerns that prompted the circle, including any miscommunications and definitions of toxicity." Prompts might include sharing instances of misunderstanding or reflecting on impactful quotes, like Steve Maraboli's: "Take accountability. Blame is the water in which many dreams and relationships drown."

A powerful advocate of joy (whose hashtag is *Nothing Can Steal My Joy*), Yomi uses circles to focus on shifts to healing harm and crafting meaningful solutions as "participants are encouraged to make personal commitments toward contributing to a more positive work environment. These steps are integral in transforming the circle into a conduit for healing and positive change, ultimately benefiting both individuals and the organizational culture."

There are a number of resources available for using circles with youth. Here, our colleague Tiffani Kenney shares an approach that she uses, which provides unique insight into bridging generational differences.

4 - Tiffani's Circles for Education and Bridging Generations

Tiffani Kenney, a DEI Practitioner and Educator who is part of our belonging and inclusion team at PBS, provides insights for using circles with children. She says that "every child benefits from human connection, and there is no better way to give this opportunity than with circles." According to psychiatrist Dr. Regina Pally, "Emotions connect not only the mind and body of one individual but minds and bodies between individuals." Tiffani says that "circles create opportunities for youth to develop skills like emotional intelligence, discipline, leadership, and patience, among many other competencies. And the best thing about circles is they can be held in many spaces. Classrooms, after-school clubs, faith groups, and impromptu family discussions can all be held in circle."

As an educator, Tiffani held circles bi-weekly in her secondary school classroom. These events, called "family meetings" by her students, were a way "to pause, review expectations, empathize with each other, and reconnect as a class when we got too far from our goal." It also created a chance for them to hear her but also hear each other. The talking pieces used were different books her English class read, which helped the students focus.

Tiffani shared that the students "got to see each other for who they are but more importantly where they are." Circles were also an opportunity for students to see her "as a human and member of the class" because she served as the Circle Keeper who also participated in the circle.

"The prompts often focused on things like what they were dealing with in their lives, topics from our texts, and goals and aspirations they personally held. These circles helped us share our journeys, heal after classroom interactions, and most importantly, build community." Tiffani says circles help bridge the gap between generational differences: "It is believed that Generation Z does not want to communicate, but they just prefer to have something concrete to talk about. My students regularly were disappointed to enter the room and find we were not having 'family meeting' because it brought them comfort and they felt supported in circle. When used effectively, all generations can benefit from circles and the power they bring."

Another type of circle that helps provide education across generations are cultural intelligence circles, which Nandar Win Kerr, DEI practitioner and consultant for PBS, conducts.

5 - Nandar's Cultural Intelligence Circles

Nandar Win Kerr raises the importance of cultural intelligence circles to enhance understanding of various cultures, improve communications, and engage with curiosity and humility. When Nandar arrived as a student at St. Cloud State University in Minnesota from Yangon, Myanmar, she noticed cultural divisions at the school. To better understand how to bridge the gap, she conducted a survey among students, staff, and faculty to identify barriers to fuller integration, and a consistent answer emerged: "A lack of cultural understanding leads to fear of humiliating or offending the 'other.'" She says, "Acknowledging my curiosity with humility helps me to manage the stress of living as an immigrant and non-native English speaker in diverse cultural environments with unfamiliar cues," which cultural intelligence circles support.

Here are some prompts that Nandar suggests using in circle:

-   What does cultural intelligence mean to you, and why is it important in today's globalized world?
-   Describe a time when cultural differences presented a communication challenge and how you navigated it.
-   How do you build cultural awareness in your life?
-   How has technology impacted your experience with cross-cultural communications?

Nandar also suggests using cultural intelligence circles as a tool to educate across cultures. Here are some tips that can be shared during these circles as part of the opening or closing:

-   Embrace the power of humble listening.
-   Commit to conversations that bridge divides.
-   Be open, transparent, and willing to admit mistakes.
-   Acknowledge cultural aspects you are unfamiliar with.
-   Remind yourself that you are trying.
-   Respect yourself and avoid self-shame of your inabilities.
-   Remember that cross-cultural communication requires dialogue, not debate.
-   When your intellect fails you, show your heart.

Ultimately, cultural intelligence circles aim to establish greater self-awareness, relationship management, appreciation, and peace, which are also demonstrated through peacemaking circles. Peacemaking Circles, which are commonly used, provide a basic structure for resolving any type of conflict.

6 - Peacemaking Circles

Peacemaking Circles are a way of bringing people together in which everyone is respected, and the spiritual and emotional aspects of individual experiences are welcomed as in all circles. These circles can be used for decision-making, reconciling disagreements, addressing an experience that resulted in harm, and team building. In Peacemaking Circles, guidelines are important in governing how participants will conduct themselves in circle. Guidelines are not rules but are used as reminders to participants about their agreement to maintain certain conduct in order to create a safe space for courageous conversations. Decisions in Peacemaking Circles are made by consensus, which requires that participants be willing to adhere to decisions and support their implementation. To build a strong container, discussing values and creating guidelines are imperative.

Also known as Conflict Circles, resolution can take shape through a consensus agreement. Peacemaking Circles are being used in a variety of contexts. In neighborhoods, they provide support for those harmed by crime and help decide sentences for those who commit crimes. In schools, they create a positive classroom climate and resolve behavior problems. In the workplace, they help address conflict, and in social services, they develop more organic support systems for people struggling to get their lives together.

Because of the numerous ways to describe conflict, including a failure of collaboration, a boundary violation, or even advocacy for change in a system that has outlived its usefulness, conflict is not simply viewed as a disagreement but an opportunity for understanding, growth, learning, or generally improved relationships. As Christina Baldwin says in *Calling the Circle*, "[p]reconflict bonding is sweet, but not as potent as post conflict bonding. The circle that has lost its innocence by coming through crisis with respect for each other and the process is a circle to be reckoned with."

Baldwin says, "Getting into conflict and confusion is commonplace; what was uncommon was how we got out. Because we could agree to maintain silent until we felt spiritually directed to speak, we were able to find our way back to the center and collectively ask: 'What does Spirit want to have happen here, and how may I/we help?'"

The way that we solve conflict and bring about a peaceful solution is key. In circle, there is an environment that is more authentic and thus encourages greater transparency and trust. Change may not take place in one circle, though it might.

The most important thing is that each person in the circle takes responsibility for asking the circle for the support they want and need. Baldwin says, "[a]sking for what we need allows us to avoid power struggles and drama as ways of getting attention. This applies both to asking for technical support in the midst of a task and to asking for interpersonal support in the midst of a meeting." Each person takes responsibility for agreeing or not agreeing to participate in specific requests.

Circles do not allow us to be gatekeepers; they force us to tell our truth and to listen to the views of others. Circles do not allow us to create a narrative; they force us to be accountable to our truth and to seek resolutions that cannot be obfuscated by shame. Oftentimes, people just want to be heard, and circles allow us to hear one another through our differences.

The Circle Way says that "[m]ost human conflicts arise from a passion that has not had space to be fully expressed or witnessed by the other side." But the structure of circles gives us enough space and opportunity so that conflicting views loosen their attachments to their position, as we listen to each other with curiosity and compassion, withholding judgment.

Circles give us the vision to see beyond the walls that block us. We trust each other to be passionate and respectful. We can remain authentic without threatening the stability of the container. Racial healing presents the sort of conflict that won't be resolved with one circle, but circles will increase understanding and awareness that otherwise would not be present.

Veronica Agard, Founder of Ancestors in Training™, "examines how to apply the lessons of the past as a means to shape a better present and future for those who come after us."

6 - Veronica's Ancestors in Training™ Circles

Ancestors in Training™ is "an educational project and lived experience that centers sacred traditions, new technologies, intergenerational healing, and grief work" founded by poet, writer, community educator, and circle keeper Veronica Agard. Her Circles "allow all those who enter the circle to leave with a better sense of self and how they relate to the world."

The main agreement in Ancestors in Training™ Circles is: "What's shared here stays here, and what's learned here leaves here." Then, they open the space with an interactive question on a collaborative virtual board, which allows folks to be creative with their responses to questions, such as: "What ancestors are you bringing into this space? How are you tending to your joy? What practices do you engage in to remind you of your wholeness?" Participants are then invited to respond or react to what resonates with them.

Afterwards, the Ancestors in Training™ team continues to facilitate based on the given topic, until the healing-through-writing segment of the session. Participants are given four or five prompts that allow them to dive deeper into the topic and write their responses over the course of 20 minutes. Participants are then invited to share their written reflections with the group, disclosing as much information as they feel comfortable with.

To close the container, Veronica often shares a poem or a prayer. Attendees are given access to the session materials, including a syllabus afterward so that they can continue their journey as Ancestors in Training™.

Like the Ancestors in Training™ Circles, Nicholas Macaluso's Achilles Community Circles also create a space for deep self-reflection and healing through both the messages we receive from others and the messages we tell ourselves.

7 - Nicholas's Achilles Community Circles

Achilles Community, founded by somatic therapist Nicholas Macaluso, is a community of men (i.e., anyone who identifies as a man, cis-man, trans-man, or male) committed to reclaiming their full humanity, and coaches (of any gender) who are trained in principles of somatic therapy and anti-fragile space-holding.

Nicholas recognized that in this society, "When being a man means being strong, superior, and stoic, then it also means being less human. The harm men endure from the rites of passage through manhood robs them of their human need for vulnerability, intimacy, and safety. It conditions them into abusive relationships with themselves, those around them, and their environments. Although there may be benefits to their endurance of pain, men must engage in psycho-emotional healing practices to restore their relationship with their humanity and the humanity of others." The Achilles Community offers integrative personal training and emotional wellness support circles, where men can share what they're going through, connect with those who have similar experiences, and gain valuable support to strengthen their relationship with themselves and others.

The support circles are "anti-fragile" in that they are "both sanctuaries for men to rest and be held, as well as training grounds for them to grow and be pushed." They "believe the restoration of a man's humanity requires him to experience the beneficial risks of vulnerability . . . . In our circles, we practice the embodiment of a resilient vulnerability that experiences cohesive growth as a result of stress, tension, injury, or resistance."

These are some prompts used in Achilles Community Circles:
- Can you genuinely express your emotions while maintaining empathy and compassion for yourself and the person you are communicating with? If yes, how? If no, why not?

- Are you willing to be vulnerable at the risk of experiencing discomfort, stress, pain, or even potential injury? Why or why not?
- Can you discern being (psycho-emotionally) unsafe from being (psycho-emotionally) uncomfortable? If yes, how? If no, why not?
- When you don't feel psycho-emotionally safe, what are some things you need to restore your safety?

Powerful circles are also held during women's conferences and summits, where women share personal stories of courage, connection, and commitment to helping themselves and other women succeed. When we lean into truth, it does not permit fragility, regardless of background or gender. True circles require that we be uncomfortable in order to rediscover ourselves beyond the realm of discomfort.

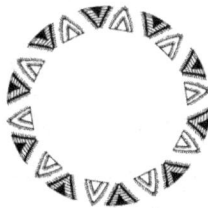

8 - Women Summit Circles

At FDNY, our belonging and inclusion team led a Women's Summit every year welcoming women and their allies across New York City to gather and celebrate the power, talents, accomplishments, aspirations, and commitment in support of one another. The day-long summit consisted of activities uplifting women in community such as positive affirmations, inspirational presentations, participation in women's activism projects, physical exercises led by women firefighters, leadership panel discussions, and circles. We held breakout circles so participants could get to know one another and share their reflections on wisdom throughout the day's activities.

Sometimes, each breakout circle was led by one or two circle keepers who shared a quick breathing exercise as an opening, circle guidelines, and then a round of introductions in which participants shared their name, the organization they worked for, and one word that described how they were feeling. These safe spaces to express oneself as a woman should not be confused with the safety or fragility of just being nice, but standing on the shoulders of truth to invoke the power of who we are with strength and conviction.

Prompts included: What is your story of courage? What is your story of compassion? What is one self-care practice you honor? What is one way you are supportive of other women? Participants also shared one takeaway that they could apply in their professional/personal lives. The circles concluded with a closing practice where participants took three deep breaths together. The women's summit circles helped create a space where women can have meaningful conversations, encourage each other to excel in all aspects of life, and form friendships that will last a lifetime.

Nine PBS is another organization that has integrated circles into their work so that people can come together in a space of unity, support, and shared experiences.

9 – Kate's Organization-wide Circles

Nine PBS, a PBS member station in St. Louis, Missouri, holds restorative circles every month with the entire staff invited to attend. Kate Midgett, Nine PBS's Vice President and Chief Organizational Excellence Officer, explains that the circles start with the Keeper introducing the ground rules and purpose of the group, especially if it's the first time attending for some so that everyone understands the expectations. Stones with words inscribed on them are used as talking pieces. Depending on the circle topic, the stone could have any of the following words: rest, hope, family, support, laughter, energy, serenity, healing, comfort, etc.

The Keeper introduces the first prompt and why it's an important question for the group. Kate says, "We always begin with something related to work. For example, 'how do you maintain a sense of serenity when work obligations become demanding?' In this case, we would use the serenity stone as the talking piece, passing it around the circle, enabling everyone to respond." Kate shares that the next prompt introduced is usually more personal such as, "What does serenity look like for you when you are feeling emotionally healthy?"

Nine PBS circles end with each participant stating one word that describes what they have gained from the shared experiences of others around them.

Numerous other types of circles can be used in the workplace and in other spaces for multiple purposes with various configurations.

10 - Other Types of Circles

We use several other types of circles, including the following:

Coaching Circle: Cecilia designed Coaching Circles to provide coaching through storytelling. Although group coaching can be used, we've used three people to teach principles that are useful for coaching, like the creation of values, purpose, leadership philosophy, authentic leadership, and other key principles for positive and appreciative leadership that apply to everyone.

Stick Circle: Learned from Planning Change, a stick circle introduces the use of sticks for nonverbal communication rounds. These are some of the most powerful circles that cause us to dig deep to express what's on our minds and in our hearts. Anywhere from 20-30 sticks of different sizes gathered from nature are passed to each person, who use them in any way they want. Then, the sticks are gathered and handed to the next person in the circle, together as a talking piece.

Laughter Circle: A laughter circle introduces aspects that require laughter. Laughter can increase in tone; be used at the beginning and/or end; and welcome silence. Participants can move around the room, shake, jump, dance, feel silly, and engage play as part of their expressions in circle.

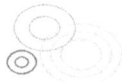

Appreciation Circle: An appreciation or gratitude circle allows us a space to uplift appreciation for circle participants or for whatever someone feels grateful for. This can be done through prompts or by directing all shares to one circle participant.

Team Meeting Circle: The type of circle that we use most frequently are team meeting circles, which are team meetings conducted in circle, providing a structure that ensures that all participants' ideas, concerns, questions, achievements, and challenges can be heard. The manager can be the circle keeper for the first team meeting circle to role model the format and encourage other team members to be circle keepers for subsequent circles so that all team members have an opportunity to demonstrate their leadership abilities.

Openings and closings can include quotes, stories, excerpts from articles or books, poems, videos, etc.

Prompts can include:

- What is one accomplishment from this month that you're proud of?
- What project do you need support from other team members on?
- How are you maintaining work-life balance this week?

Regardless of what type of circle you design, as long as it is done with grace, it will be effective in bringing about the change that you desire.

Regardless of what type of circle you do, circles are "never about persuasion. They are a process of exploring meaning from each perspective . . . [P]articipants may find common ground or understand ... why another person sees something differently. The more diverse the perspectives . . . the richer the dialogue."

Carolyn Boyes-Watson, *et al.*,
from *Circle Forward*

CHAPTER 12

Cultivating Change

Circles move beyond talking,
to grace walking,
strengthening hope,
envisioning possibilities,
radiating respect,
sealing love,
cultivating change.

D avid Ausberger, a Mennonite minister, once said, "Being heard is so close to being loved that for the average person, they are almost indistinguishable." The compassion that we feel by being heard in circles is fueled by a unique connection to "all our relations" and the stories that continue to live through truth-telling. Circles provide a vital catalyst to touch where it hurts, to hold our anger and pain, and to build a container for change to be born. Circles help us build a community of resilience. In *Real Change*, Sharon Salzberg shares that when we respond to "our own pain with more presence and compassion, the energy we have for responding to the pain of others increases dramatically, as does our sense of connection and care."

As the author Barry Lopez once said, "Sometimes a person needs a story more than food to stay alive. That is why we put these stories in each other's memory. This is how people care for themselves." When we make storytelling through circles a practice, this vehicle for expression evolves from being more than just an occasional tool for courageous conversations and becomes instrumental to how we change for the better. Centering in circle is a lot like a prayer—not because we are asking for something but because we are lifting our consciousness in the highest frequency of receptivity. By listening, we feed one of our most important needs, which is the inevitability of change.

If meditation is the highest form of prayer, circle is the highest form of dialogue. Being present to listen without judgment in circle allows us to hear more than what comes up for ourselves; circles are also a sanctuary for embracing what comes up for others. Authenticity is vital because if we don't feel safe enough to be ourselves, we won't have the capacity to honor the truth in others. In circle, we cultivate change together through the practice of speaking our truth and listening to the truth shared by others—no matter how difficult.

Because we share our truth with humility and listen deeply in circle, we cultivate the psychological safety that is necessary for our success. Participants share stories from the heart and listen with an openness that is bigger than egos. The circle is a container of psychological safety, accepting whoever shows up with power and purpose (inclusion safety), sharing whatever truth we need to learn from the experiences that others share (learner safety), contributing with courage that is honored with the silence of appreciation (contributor safety), and challenging the status quo with the grace encouraged by our stories (challenger safety). As set forth above, this framework of psychological safety was developed by Dr. Timothy Clark in his book, *The 4 Stages of Psychological Safety*.

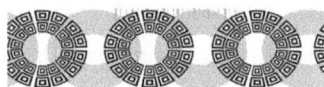

These four aspects of psychological safety can be explained by a framework of positive and appreciative leadership. We all have agency, which is another way of saying that we all have the power and purpose to choose how we can make a difference in the lives of others. Power doesn't mean the acquisition of things, the accumulation of titles, or the assertion of control over others. Power means that everything we do and every way we treat ourselves and others is the result of our choice.

Circles allow us to go within, focusing on the leader we choose to be, starting by leading ourselves because we are the most challenging person to lead.

Circles Allow Us to Fully Express Our Power

When we come together to listen to one another, we witness the power shared by others through their purpose, gifts, and talents, as well as their basic right to belong. Circles are important in cultivating change because they allow us to speak from the "I," and all people have a need for freedom and autonomy.

According to change management experts, we like to feel that our actions are driven by us rather than the whims of others. Circles ask participants how they feel and what they want to do rather than tell them, which is one of the best ways to encourage change. We speak with power into the unlimited space that circles offer to hold our vision. When we give answers to questions, they reflect our truth, help us commit to what we share, and reinforce our accountability to one another. In circle, we have more accountability in discerning our values, our purpose in life, and even our leadership philosophy.

Circles Provide the Trust and Transparency to Learn

Change is hard because people overvalue what they have, own, or are doing already. In *The Catalyst: How to Change Anyone's Mind*, Wharton Professor Jonah Berger teaches that we resist change because it is costly to the brain: Learning something new uses more resources and energy than relying on the automatic processes involved in habitual activity. We become attached to what we know, but circles invite us to lean into what we don't know.

An important part of learning is being able to make a mistake. As women of color, Cecilia and Gina both realize the consequences of mistakes being made by people who are marginalized as opposed to those in a "dominant caste." Generally, society doesn't give everyone a broad license to make mistakes and correct them. In the *Right Kind of Wrong: The Science of Failing Well*, Amy Edmondson teaches that everyone is entitled to an equal license to fail. Learning safety is an environment that provides an equal license for all to learn by taking risks and even by failing first to succeed.

Circles provide a license to fail by building strong connections through bonding, team building, communication, and compassion. We have seen the benefits of circle reverberate throughout organizations with more lasting support, strengthened ties of empathy, and trust. This is an example of the connection that Sarah Lewis references in *Positive Psychology and Change: How Leadership, Collaboration, and Appreciative Inquiry Create Transformational Results*: "Communicating with others creates connection that allows us to stay informed, as well as provides the value of our own input, making better decisions for ourselves and others."

When we participate in circles with courage, we can be more vulnerable because there is no judgment. We can be courageous enough to not know because what we offer is the deep core of who we are, building trust through the authenticity of our own truth. Sharing truth invites us to see each other in a new way, beyond the masks we wear and the code-switching we use as we courageously remember and introduce who we really are. When we can appreciate who we are, we begin to interact with others more genuinely, building and sustaining relationships that provide more support beyond circles.

Circles Help Us Appreciate Our Contributions

Circles provide a respected space to contribute our ideas, which also helps cultivate change. The more we share our ideas in circle, the more they are cherished, which is important because circles may be the rare instance where all voices are invited, heard, and valued. Dr. Clark says that despite their "ability to do the job, an individual may nonetheless be denied contributor safety, because of the arrogance or insecurity of the leader, personal or institutional bias, prejudice or discrimination, prevailing team norms that reinforce insensitivity, a lack of empathy, or aloofness." This prejudice even occurs in organizations that are supportive of diversity, especially if the diversity is merely to reach recruitment goals or to respond to what is happening in the world around us (*e.g.*, the murder of George Floyd and others) rather than to support the ability of all employees to contribute their unique experiences and outlooks. Circles support the learning opportunities necessary for all to value diverse views, expressions, visions, and insights.

Circles allow us to share compassion and genuine appreciation for the contributions of those from all backgrounds, which is the true purpose of diversity. Circles plant the seeds of cooperation, catalysts that help create a work environment that not only welcomes everyone but also builds and strengthens a container that is strong enough to hold differences of opinion. In circle, we can pause and feel reverence for the creativity nurtured by a variety of ideas.

Circles Help Provide the Grace for Cultivating Change

Circles are a vehicle for cultivating positive change with grace. Dr. Clark calls this "challenger safety," but circles recognize that challenge is not the only important aspect of cultivating change. Grace is also required to cultivate change. The challenge is not about blame, shame, or guilt but the courage to be vulnerable enough to speak our truth while deeply listening to the ideas of others. The grace that creates a safe space for challenging norms is also an acronym: G – Growing in Self-Awareness; R – Regulating Ourselves Beyond Triggers; A – Assessing Challenges with Empathy; C – Centering with Humility; and E – Evolving with Pro-Social Behavior. When we are compassionate about the need to change and the way we manage it, we are better able to work together on ideas that will result in lasting success.

As Jonah Berger says in *The Catalyst: How to Change Anyone's Mind*, we resist change because our brain is wired to perceive it as a threat, especially if it is unexpected. Change creates a contagious, negative spiral of emotion, and brain resources get rerouted to basic survival functions, releasing anger and fear. Circles provide a safe space for not only looking outward but also seeing inward so that we do not complain but take responsibility for working with others to cultivate change. Circles also contribute to change as a process, allowing for a stronger root cause analysis and building consensus on positive and negative aspects of a challenge before co-creating a solution.

For any change, circles allow those at every level of an organization to be heard, giving executive teams opportunities to bond, and positioning them to succeed in their work together. One of the most powerful uses of circles is when leaders of organizations are courageous enough to role model them from the top. Circles also provide a mechanism for input to be heard throughout every level of the organization. As Chapter 11 shows, we can design circles to support every aspect of our journey. To cultivate change, we can use a variety of circles as a mechanism to develop our vision as well as strengthen our commitment to change. Thus, circles provide a meaningful forum for top executives, as well as staff, to use for collaboration.

Circles are a valuable tool for assessing the cultural landscape and can help jump-start cultural change. When there are emotionally charged events like racial, ethnic, sexual, or other types of violence motivated by prejudice, legislative or court decisions dismantling proactive programs, or even positive historical or social events, circles can help empower us to act affirmatively to work together in bringing about the change that we need. It may be easy to stick to the status quo when all seems well because change is costly and requires effort. However, when dismantlement threatens the good of all, circles are a starting place to move us beyond our comfort zones to do the work that must be done.

Circles never end really, and once formed, serve as a continuous opportunity to connect. Thus, there are ways to seal the circle process in a manner that respects the sacredness of the stories shared and blesses the contributions of all present but leave open the possibility of returning to a safe space to reflect whenever necessary. Circles provide a communal pause on how to process the present moment, a way to both engage and disengage from it and apply what we have learned before we return to our responsibilities outside of circle.

When we align with our purpose and honor the situations we are in with grace, we are inspired by solutions that challenge us to grow and evolve with new ideas. The creative process is ignited when our level of psychological safety is so high that we can see beyond the status quo and leave our comfort zones by taking risks that reward us with the innovation of change. Belonging and inclusion are important to embracing all our stories regardless of race, gender, creed, age, ethnicity, socio-economic status, geography, sexual orientation, veteran status, disability, etc., which are the prism through which collective wisdom shines with visions that are so amazing, they not only heal old wounds but also build new avenues of inspiration.

We open and close circles with the most powerful energy that there is: love. Love is not a weakness but a strength that enhances our capabilities, relationships, and achievements. Circles are a catalyst for change, removing roadblocks and lowering the barriers that keep people guarded. When we try to change minds or even organizations in the world, we're often so focused on ourselves and our desired outcome that we spend all our energy thinking about the various ways we could push people in that direction. But in doing so, we tend to forget about the person whose mind we're trying to change and what's stopping them. Circles permit us to listen to what is important to others and get to the root of the issues we are facing.

In circles, we can reflect on all the lessons we have learned and how we've changed through the process. Circles are without limit: healing, educating, guiding, witnessing, prophesizing, resolving, connecting, building, and co-creating the magic that is always present. As Kay Pranis shares, we "have only begun to scratch the surface of ways" that circles "change the content and meaning of our lives. We are limited only by our imaginations, our willingness to be in a respectful and loving relationship with every part of creation, and our ability to allow the pattern of the Circle to emerge without trying to manage or control it."

So, how do we conclude a circle without diminishing its effectiveness after a circle session concludes? At the end of our circle certification courses, participants don't want the circle process to end. How are we able to strengthen the healing glue of connection long after we've departed from the physical experience of circle but not from the ever-abiding presence of its spirit? Is it merely a function of holding the struggle, pain, and peace of those with whom we share the vulnerability and compassion of belonging, or something else?

At minimum, we close the circle with a poem, a story, a video, a prayer, a word, or a quote of truth that summarizes what is important to us, as well as provide the tools that strengthen us with greater resilience. Book excerpts, silence, one-word check-outs, and so many other different closings can be used, including those we co-create, like those in Cecilia's book *Unbroken Circles: Holding Space, Finding Forgiveness, Transcending Edges,* a collection of poetry used for circle openings or closings.

Our favorite way to close is the lovingkindness meditation, which Sharon Salzberg has provided many resources on, shared in our list of Resources following this chapter. In her book, *Lovingkindness: The Revolutionary Act of Happiness*, Sharon says we "dissolve the concepts of separateness that have ruled our lives by practicing *metta* for all beings without exception. Lovingkindness for all beings is the foundation of moral and spiritual awakening... Those looking for silence, for the end of the conditioning of self and other, for profound transformation, need to look at the power of developing love for all." Similarly, in his book *Fidelity: How to Create a Loving Relationship That Lasts*, Thích Nhất Hanh says, "[i]n true love, you don't exclude anyone. . . . Loving one person is an opportunity to love everyone. The deepest gift mindfulness can bring is the wisdom of nondiscrimination." Circles support nondiscrimination, which allows us to build community while uplifting the well-being of the entire world. In essence, every circle is a container of love.

As we close this circle of love, the circle of this book that we've shared, we realize that the time we spent together is not coincidental. We know that we are always in our right place, at our right time. We appreciate how you have listened to our stories, as well as shared some of your own. We value how you will use this important tool of honoring the stories of others to build an even stronger community and more cohesive teams by your own circles of openness, transparency, and trust. We seal our circle with faith that we can return to and find ourselves at the threshold of a new awakening again, and again, and again. Circles are a continuum of infinity and, like all important change, they are a journey that never ends.

So here, right now, we leave you with *metta*, chosen by us as the lasting glue of our connection. *Metta* is the lovingkindness that appreciates who we are, in whichever way that has brought us to this moment.

Pause and tell yourself how much you love your life experience. If it is difficult, take a moment, and write yourself a love letter listing at least twelve attributes that you love about your life journey.

Gina receives the talking piece from Cecilia, and shares with gratitude the twelve attributes of her life's journey that she loves:

1 – her caring parents and parental figures who instilled in her the importance of following her dreams; 2 – her Chinese heritage that she is proud to discover more about each day; 3 – that her life experiences have taught her fluent Greek, which enabled her to become curious about other cultures and really see us all as one people; 4 – that the Peace Corps and YMCA broadened her horizons, granting her opportunities to serve the global community; 5 – that NYU allowed her to design her own graduate

program at NYU in DEI; 6 – that all the DEI leaders she has met, and has yet to meet, are dedicated to helping one another and this world to be a better place for all; 7 – that her experience with the United Nations taught her that you can never be too young to have your voice heard and make a difference; 8 – that she has the most supportive family and friends who are always there to support her through all the highs and lows, including her loving partner, Barish; 9 - that she has enhanced belonging and inclusion at FDNY in the city where she grew up; 10 – that she is making significant contributions at PBS, an organization she has always admired and could not be prouder to be part of; 11 – that Mrs. Torres introduced her to circles in her fifth grade class; 12 – that Cecilia's visionary, inspirational, and appreciative leadership brought circles to FDNY, where Gina first became a Circle Keeper and grew as a belonging and inclusion leader. Gina then passes the talking piece to Cecilia.

When Cecilia receives the talking piece, she shares with gratitude the twelve attributes of her life's journey that she loves:

1 – the fact that she was born to parents who had infinite love to breathe into her as a "Loving"; 2 – that in her birthplace, the inner city of Detroit, the experience of being African American is a powerful under-current of strength; 3 – that she grew up with four brothers who taught her the joy of storytelling and how to fight for justice; 4 – that Cass Technical High School taught her that genius is the province of everyone; 5 – that her speech coach Mrs. Hamburger helped her get a National Competitive

Scholarship to Howard University, where she created its first major in Theater Management; 6 – that she was selected for UCLA's theater and film graduate management program where she focused on producing diverse content; 7 – that she followed her calling to be an attorney, which gave her another way to solve challenges; 8 – that she heeded her calling to be a minister upon graduating from NY Theological Seminary and was ordained to support a holistic culture of inclusion in the workplace; 9 – that she created Spiritmuv, a not-for-profit church devoted to spiritual development; 10 – that she founded Myrtle Tree Press in 2002, in honor of her mother, to publish her mother's books for children; 11 – that she left law to build FDNY's Diversity and Inclusion Office, hiring Gina as her first graduate intern, who later became FDNY's first DEI Manager; 12 – that she moved to Virginia from Brooklyn, with her amazing husband Rev. Marlon Cromwell, to lead DEI for PBS, one of America's greatest stewards of storytelling, working with such amazing leaders as CEO Paula Kerger, as well as Jonathan, Sylvia, Sara, Susi, Jeremy, Jill, Rhonda, Mike, Katherine, Scott, Brian, Ira, Tom, Andrea, Tia, Tiffani, Kourtney, Carolyn, Rachelle, Poonam, Lisa, Talisha, Diane, Judith, Amanda, Kai, Schenika, JoAnna, Lauren, Raisa, Sharon, Sarah, Jared, Gabino, Rahlana, Gabe, Ingrid, Iko, Janet, Mary, Danielle, Nandar, Liz, Thomas, Toanya, Valentia, Jason, Maribel, Diana, Deanna, Gabbi, Adam, Adaora, Christopher, Jess, Nandini, Paula, Lori, Crystal, Caitlin, Tania, Max, Maria, Laura, Jennifer, Hana, Megan, Amy, Francine, Theo, Kelsey, Jim, Nathan, Kate, Timothy, Eric, Yemisi, Beryl, Eugenia, Stephen, Whitney, Iris, Veronica, Shay, Joyce, Shayna, David,

Blanca, and others too numerous to name because of space, who work or have worked closely with both she and Gina as they continue to teach, grow and lead powerful circles as vehicles of change.

The next thing that we must do as part of our *metta* meditation is send love to everyone who reads this book as well as those met on the highways and byways of life who contributed to its content, and to those easy for us to love like all of our relatives and friends and our first responders like FDNY—people who put their lives on the line every moment of the day to save others; and to our PBS family who have remained committed to providing a trusted window to the world for over 50 years.

We then send peace to those who are difficult to love, personally, nationally, and worldwide, releasing fear with hope and the power of knowing that we are the change that we seek, realizing that circles are a timeless tool to open numerous hearts with the courage of unity rather than the cowardice of hate.

Finally, we send love to the entire nation, planet, and infinite galaxies within the universe, which always conspire to help us.

Then, and only then, Beloved, is our circle closed.

RESOURCES

Augsburger, David W., *Caring Enough to Hear and Be Heard* (1982).

Baldwin, Christina, *Calling the Circle* (1994).

Baldwin, Christina & Linnea, Ann, *The Circle Way* (1987).

Berger, Jonah, *The Catalyst* (2020).

Boyes-Watson, Carolyn, *Peacemaking Circles and Urban Youth* (2008).

Boyes-Watson, Carolyn & Pranis, Kay, *Circle Forward* (2020).

Boyes-Watson, Carolyn & Pranis, Kay, *Heart of Hope* (2010).

Brach, Tara, *Radical Acceptance* (2023).

Brach, Tara, *Radical Compassion* (2019).

Brach, Tara, "How do we bridge the divides?" (Nov. 29, 2023). www.youtube.com/watch?v=NKoaTklkNnw.

Brach, Tara, "What is our Refuge in the Midst of Crisis? A Conversation with Tara Brach and Stephen Fulder" (Oct. 6, 2023). www.youtube.com/watch?v=ZTBfViEYTuM&t=168s

Brookes, Derek R., *Beyond Harm* (2019).

Brother Lawrence, *The Practice of the Presence of God* (1994).

Brown, Brené, "How to be vulnerable at work without spilling everything," TED (Mar. 1, 2021). https://ideas.ted.com/how-to-be-vulnerable-at-work-without-spilling-everything-from-brene-brown/

Brown, Brené, "3 Things You Can Do to Stop a Shame Spiral," *Oprah's Lifeclass*, OWN (Oct. 6, 2013). www.youtube.com/watch?v=TdtabNt4S7E.

Brown, Brené, "Shame Is Lethal," *Super Soul Sunday*, OWN (Mar. 24, 2013). www.youtube.com/watch?v=GEBjNv5M784.

Brown, Brené, "Listening to Shame," TED (Mar. 16, 2012). https://www.youtube.com/watch?v=psN1DORYYV0.

Brown, Brené, "The Power of Vulnerability," TED (Jan. 3, 2011). www.youtube.com/watch?v=iCvmsMzlF70.

Brown, Brené, *The Gifts of Imperfection* (2010).

Burns, Catherine, *All These Wonders* (2017).

Cahill, Sedonia & Halpern, Joshua, *The Ceremonial Circle* (1992).

Ciaramicoli, Arthur P. & Ketcham, Katherine, *The Power of Empathy* (2000).

Clark, Timothy, *The 4 Stages of Psychological Safety* (2020).

Cohen, Johnathan, *The Naming of America: Fragments We've Shored Against Ourselves* (1988). www.jonathancohen-web.com/america.html.

Courageous Conversations on Racial Inclusion (2020). https://online.flippingbook.com/view/698609469/

Coyle, Daniel, *The Culture Code* (2018).

Davis, Aida Mariam, "The Problem with Tables," *Stanford Social Innovation Review* (2022). https://doi.org/10.48558/JY4W-G212

Davis, Fania E., *The Little Book of Race and Restorative Justice* (2019).

DeAngelis, Tori, "Want to boost your mental health? Take a Walk," *Amer. Psych. Ass'n* (2022). www.apa.org/monitor/2022/11/defeating-depression-naturally.

DeWolf, Thomas Norman & Geddes, Jodie, *The Little Book of Racial Healing* (2019).

Duhigg, Charles, "What Google Learned from Its Quest to Build the Perfect Team," *The New York Times* (2016). www.nytimes.com/2016/02/28/magazine/what-google-learned-from-its-quest-to-build-the-perfect-team.html.

Eastman, Owen, *Belonging: The Ancient Code of Togetherness* (2023).

Ebner, Kate & Martens, Izzy, *Holding Space* (2022).

Edmondson, Amy C., *Right Kind of Wrong: The Science of Failing Well* (2023).

Edmondson, Amy C., *The Fearless Organization* (2018).

Engel, Beverly, *Women Circling the Earth* (2000).

Frederickson, Barbara, *Positivity* (2009).

Garfield, Charles & Spring, Cindy, *Wisdom Circles* (1998).

"Genetics vs. Genomics Fact Sheet," National Human Genome Research Institute (2018).

Goleman, Daniel, *Emotional Intelligence* (2006).

Gorman, Amanda, *The Hill We Climb* (2021).

Greenwald, Anthony. G., & Banaji, Mahzarin. R, "Implicit social cognition: Attitudes, self-esteem, and stereotypes," *Psychological Review* (1995).

Hanh, Thích Nhât, *Fidelity* (2011).

Hanh, Thích Nhât, *Living Buddha, Living Christ* (2007).

Hanh, Thích Nhât & Lingo, Kaira Jewel, *Together We Are One* (2006).

Helmich, Portland, "How radical listening can heal division—and why it matters now more than ever," Kripalu (June 1, 2020).

Hougaard, Rasmus & Carter, Jacqueline, *Compassionate Leadership* (2022).

Kang, Yoona, *et al.*, "The Nondiscriminating Heart: Lovingkindness Meditation Training Decreases Implicit Intergroup Biases," *Journal of Experimental Psychology* (2013).

Kelley, Tim, *True Purpose* (2009).

Kimmerer, Robin Wall, *Braiding Sweetgrass* (2013).

King, Martin Luther, Jr., *Where Do We Go from Here?* (1986).

King, Ruth, *Mindful of Race* (2018).

Landone, Brown, *Soul Catalysts and How to Use Them* (1939).

Lewis, Sarah, *Positive Psychology and Change* (2016).

Loeb, Paul Rogat, *Soul of a Citizen* (1999).

Lopez, Barry, *Crow and Weasel* (1998).

Loving, Cecilia B., *Good Medicine* (2021).

Loving, Cecilia B., *The Power of Inclusion* (2021).

Loving, Cecilia B., *Unbroken Circles* (2020).

Lewis, Sarah, *Positive Psychology and Change* (2016).

Lueke, Adam & Gibson, Bryan, "Brief Mindfulness Meditation Reduces Discrimination," *Psychology of Consciousness, Theory, Research, and Practice* (2015).

Lueke, Adam & Gibson, Bryan, "Mindfulness Meditation Reduces Implicit Age and Race Bias," *Social Psychological and Personality Science* (2014).

Magee, Rhonda V., *The Inner Work of Racial Justice* (2020).

Matthieu, Ricard, *Happiness (2008)*.

McKinsey & Company, "What is psychological safety?," (2023). www.mckinsey.com/featured-insights/mckinsey-explainers/what-is-psychological-safety#.

Mehl-Madrona, Lewis, *Healing the Mind through the Power of Story* (2010).

Menakem, Resmaa, *My Grandmother's Hands* (2017).

Morrison, Toni, *The Nobel Lecture in Literature* (1993).

Myss, Caroline, *Why People Don't Heal and How They Can* (1998).

Neff, Kristin, *Self-Compassion* (2011).

Nossel, Murray, *Powered by Storytelling* (2018).

Pally, Regina, "Emotional processing; the mind-body connection," *The International Journal of Psycho-Analysis* (1998).

Phillips, Katherine W., "How Diversity Makes Us Smarter," *Scientific American* (2017).

Pranis, Kay, Chilton, Karen, *et al.*, *The Little Book of Circle Processes* (2005).

Pranis, Kay, Stuart, Barry, *et al.*, *Peacemaking Circles* (2011).

Richard, Larry, "Herding Cats: The Lawyer Personality Revealed," *LawyerBrain*.

Salzberg, Sharon, *Real Change* (2020).

Salzberg, Sharon, *Real Love* (2017).

Salzberg, Sharon, *Real Happiness at Work* (2014).

Salzberg, Sharon, *Lovingkindness* (2011).

Schein, Edgar, *Humble Inquiry* (2013).

Shange, Ntozake, *For Colored Girls Who Have Committed Suicide/When the Rainbow is Enuf* (1975).

Sood, Amit, *Mindfulness Redesigned for the Twenty-First Century* (2018).

Stell, Alexander & Farsides, Tom, "Brief lovingkindness meditation reduces racial bias, meditated by positive other-regarding emotions," *Motivation and Emotions* (2015).

Stevens, Shawn, "Indigenous Music and Storytelling," Kripalu (2023).

Sue, Derald Wing, *Race Talk and the Conspiracy of Silence* (2015).

Talaga, Tanya, *All Our Relations* (2018).

Tapia, Andrés T., "Diversity 2.0: The Inclusive Leader," (2019). https://focus.kornferry.com/diversity-2-0-the-inclusive-leader/.

"The Ephebic Oath," Townsend Harris High School (2023).

Tipping, Colin, *Radical Forgiveness* (2010).

Toussaint, Loren, *Forgiveness and Health* (2015).

Tutu, Desmond, *No Future Without Forgiveness* (2000).

Tutu, Desmond & Tutu, Mpho, *The Book of Forgiving* (2014).

Van Der Kolk, Bessel M.D., *The Body Keeps the Score* (2015).

Whitney, Diana D., *The Power of Appreciative Inquiry* (2010).

Wilkerson, Isabel, *Caste* (2020).

Worthington Jr., Everett, L., "The New Science of Forgiveness," *Greater Good Magazine* (2004). greatergood.berkeley.edu/article/item/the_new_science_of_forgiveness.

Yoshino, Kenji, *Covering* (2007).

Zajonc, Arthur, *Meditation as Contemplative Inquiry* (2008).

ABOUT THE AUTHORS

Cecilia B. Loving is a DEI thought leader, Circle Keeper, motivational speaker, and author, who is SVP – Head of DEI for PBS. Her work in restorative justice, storytelling, inclusive leadership, racial inclusion, mindfulness, and well-being helps redefine the importance of self-care and self-empowerment to create a positive and holistic environment for everyone. Her experience in uplifting the opportunity that belonging and inclusion present for the success of organizations includes both the private and public sectors.

Cecilia has a Juris Doctor from NYU School of Law and a Master of Divinity from NY Theological Seminary, as well as a BFA from Howard University and an MFA in Theatre Management from UCLA's School of Theatre, Film, and Television. With over 20 years of experience as a lawyer in private law firms, a background in Human Rights Law, leadership as an ordained minister, experience providing DEI leadership for both private businesses and government agencies, Cecilia combines legal, analytical, and strategic skills to co-create a positive and holistic work environment. She is a winner of the National Diversity Council's 2021 Top 100 Diversity Officers Award; the New York City Department of Citywide Administrative Services' 2021 Innovation Award for FDNY's Inclusive Culture Strategy; Lawline's Top Women Faculty of 2020 Award; the New York City Bar Association's 2020 Diversity and Inclusion Champion Award; ABC News' First Responder Friday Award, as well as several other awards.

She has written several books and numerous articles and blogs, including but not limited to the following: *The Power of Inclusion: Meditating with Compassion, Healing with Generosity, Leading with Love; Good Medicine: 100 Prayers From the Pandemic; Unbroken Circles: Holding Space, Finding Forgiveness, Transcending Edges; God is a Brown Girl Too; The Gift of Going Within; Prayers for Those Standing on the Edge of Greatness; Seeing Myself as God Sees Me;* and *God is a Lawyer Too.*

Gina Leow is a DEI thought leader, teacher, and Circle Keeper, currently serving as Director of DEI at PBS. Gina seeks to infuse both her work and her daily life with mindfulness, storytelling, design thinking, social psychology, and team-building expertise.

She received a BA in International Relations with a focus in Asian Studies from the City College of New York. Her dedication to volunteerism led her to join the Peace Corps and travel to Sichuan, China, where she instructed hundreds of college students and teachers on Teaching English as a Foreign Language. She was the NYU Gallatin School of Individualized Study's first Paul D. Coverdell Fellowship recipient and designed the school's first MA degree in DEI. She also has certifications in inclusion and belonging from Cornell, Yale, and Stanford universities.

Gina has extensive work experience in collaborative leadership, youth development, international relations, and intercultural communications with organizations such as the United Nations Association of the USA, International YMCA, FDNY, and All Stars Project. She served as Vice President for, and continues to advise, the New York City Peace Corps Association's Board of Directors. She also currently represents The Ribbon International NGO to the United Nations Department of Global Communications. Gina created the New York City Bar Association's first Mindfulness and Well-Being Toolkit and was included in Lawline's Top Women Faculty of 2020. She was named winner of the Department of Citywide Administrative Services' Innovation Award for FDNY's Inclusive Culture Strategy in 2021.

In her spare time, Gina enjoys cooking, traveling, improving her Greek and Mandarin Chinese language skills, playing board games, being a cat mom, and catching up on the latest shows and movies—especially on PBS!